UNIVERSITY CASEBOOK SERIES®

2018 SUPPLEMENT TO

EMPLOYMENT LAW

CASES AND MATERIALS

CONCISE AND UNABRIDGED EIGHTH EDITIONS

MARK A. ROTHSTEIN
Herbert F. Boehl Chair of Law and Medicine
University of Louisville

LANCE M. LIEBMAN
William S. Beinecke Professor of Law
Columbia University

KIMBERLY A. YURACKO
Dean and Judd and Mary Morris Leighton Professor of Law
Northwestern Pritzker School of Law

PAUL M. SECUNDA
Professor of Law and Director, Labor and Employment Law Program
Marquette University Law School

CHARLOTTE GARDEN
Associate Professor
Seattle University School of Law

FOUNDATION
PRESS

University Casebook Series is a trademark registered in the U.S. Patent and Trademark Office.

© 2018 LEG, Inc. d/b/a West Academic
    444 Cedar Street, Suite 700
    St. Paul, MN 55101
    1-877-888-1330

Printed in the United States of America

ISBN: 978-1-64242-609-0

TABLE OF CONTENTS

PART IV. TERMINATING THE RELATIONSHIP

TABLE OF CASES

The principal cases are in bold type.

UNIVERSITY CASEBOOK SERIES®

2018 SUPPLEMENT TO

EMPLOYMENT LAW

CASES AND MATERIALS

CONCISE AND UNABRIDGED EIGHTH EDITIONS

PART I

BACKGROUND

CHAPTER 1

WORK AND LAW

A. WORK AND SOCIETY

Page 11. Please add the following note.

1A. One way of quantifying the American Dream is to calculate the percentage of children age 30 who earned more than their parents at the same age. Using deidentified tax records, researchers made the following calculation. For children born in 1940, 92% earned more than their parents. That figure has declined steadily for children born after 1950 (79%), 1960 (72%), 1970 (71%), and 1980 (50%). David Leonhardt, The American Dream Quantified at Last, N.Y. Times, Dec. 11, 2016, at SR2.

CHAPTER 2

THE DEVELOPMENT OF EMPLOYMENT LAW

A. THE FOUNDATIONS OF EMPLOYMENT LAW

2. EMPLOYER—EMPLOYEE

Page 20. Please add the following note.

4. For an argument for reciprocal fiduciary duties of employers and employees, see Matthew T. Bodie, Employment as Fiduciary Responsibility, 105 Geo. L.J. 819 (2017).

Page 26. Please insert before 3. EMPLOYMENT AT WILL.

Keith Cunningham-Parmeter, From Amazon to Uber: Defining Employment in the Modern Economy
90 B.U.L. Rev. 1673, 1676–77, 1680–86 (2016).

Since the end of the Great Recession, U.S. businesses have aggressively engaged in a series of organizational changes–from classifying workers as independent contractors to hiring subcontractors, to utilizing staffing agencies–to delegate employment-related responsibilities to outsiders. Although the strategic use of contactors existed long before the most recent economic downturn, the Great Recession dramatically increased this trend. Regrettably for workers caught in these settings, employment law violations represent a common practice. In addition to avoiding employment liabilities, firms that hire contractors fail to contribute to essential components of America's social safety net such as Social Security and unemployment benefits. And the scope of the problem is growing. By 2020, up to forty percent of workers are projected to become contingent "pseudo-employees," many of whom will lack the ability to enforce basic workplace protections.

Given the potential cost-savings they offer, these organizational changes represent the "future of work" for which the law must account. Unfortunately, current judicial pronouncements on these issues often embrace a cabined vision of employment that shields firms from liability. This constrained understanding of employer-employee configurations ultimately limits the reach of protective statutes, thereby resulting in a misalignment between modern workplace structures and employment rights.

* * *

I.   THE RISE OF THE CONTRACTOR DEFENSE

A.   *Working but not employed*

The uniforms that many workers wear today do not necessarily reflect the identities of their actual employers. For example, the satellite television installer who drives a DirecTV-branded truck may not actually report to DirecTV. Likewise, the Westin housekeeper who cleans hotel rooms may not receive a paycheck from the hotel chain where she works. The process of "vertical integration," wherein firms generate goods and services internally, has drastically declined over the last several decades. Given the choice between producing a service in-house or buying it from outside sources, companies increasingly turn to third parties for essential services. This growing commodification of work-related tasks has birthed an entire industry of labor intermediaries who sell discrete services in individualized packages to business.

Given the low price and availability of vendor-supplied labor, many formerly self contained companies now rely on vast networks of contractors to maintain operations. For example, some hospitals and hotels assign nearly all of their operations–housekeeping, maintenance, recordkeeping, etc.–to third parties. Similarly, when Amazon recently opened a distribution center in Tennessee, it announced that 3500 of the 4500 new employees would actually work for an outside agency that contracted with Amazon. But even though Amazon may not share an official employment relationship with workers in situations like this, the company can still exert significant influence over workers' pay and working conditions by controlling the firms that formally employ them.

Unsurprisingly, these movements have caused the number of people employed by labor-only agencies to explode in recent years. Since 2010, the staffing industry has added more jobs to the U.S. economy than any other sector. While total employment in the labor market has grown by six percent since 2009, the staffing industry has grown by forty-one percent. Many of the workers involved in these arrangements are not temporary laborers at all, but rather assume the identity of "permatemps" who receive their paychecks from supplying firms while providing labor to companies that never formally employ them. Once a niche field in the 1970s that offered only short-term work in areas such as secretarial assistance, nursing help, and day labor, the temporary staffing sector now supplies labor to numerous industries. Given this expansion, many end-user companies today see "temporary" staffing agencies as permanent extensions of their human resources departments.

* * *

B.   *The Gig Economy and Independent Contractors*

No industry better exemplifies the vast expansion of independent contracting than the on-demand or "gig" economy. Rooted in an economic model in which individuals sell services to one another, online platforms help facilitate varied forms of peer-to-peer work. Although on-demand workers represent a relatively small segment of the labor force, the number of jobs in this area is increasing rapidly. Take Uber: Valued at $50 billion, Uber is the fastest-growing startup in the world. In fact, the ride-broker's growth has been so explosive that its private market value now equals that of mainstay public companies like Target and Kraft Foods. Uber claims that it "owns no vehicles" and "employs no drivers." But even as the rideshare firm denies its employer status, it adds hundreds of thousands of driver-partners to its platform each month.

Uber's ascension has devastated taxi companies in many regions. In New York City, for example, the number of rides provided by Uber jumped in two years from 300,000 to 3.5 million, while traditional cabs lost 2.1 million rides during the same period. In 2015, San Francisco's largest taxi company, Yellow Cab, filed for bankruptcy. And Uber's long-term business plan extends well beyond ridesharing. The company now delivers, or plans to deliver food (UberEats), retail goods (UberRush), and flu shots (UberHealth), offering all of these services with nonemployee labor.

Because it categorizes its "partners" as independent contractors, Uber does not extend any employment rights–including unemployment benefits, workers' compensation, or overtime–to its drivers. The rideshare firm gains immediate economic advantages from this strategy. Uber can save up to thirty percent in payroll taxes simply by classifying its drivers as nonemployees. And Uber is not the only platform taking advantage of this exempt category of workers. Indeed, the gig economy is chock-full of firms that hire independent contractors to gain similar bottom-line benefits. From Lyft drivers to TaskRabbit gardeners, many peer marketplaces categorize their workers as nonemployees.

As first glance, the classification of on-demand workers as independent contractors might seem perfectly appropriate given that workers in the industry can accept gigs whenever they choose. But the significant influence that on-demand firms have over working conditions—from setting non-negotiable wage rates, to implementing behavior codes, to "deactivating" (i.e. firing) individuals who perform poorly—reflects a more traditional employer-employee dynamic.

O'Connor v. Uber Technologies, Inc.

82 F.Supp.3d 1133 (N.D. Cal 2015).

■ EDWARD M. CHEN, DISTRICT JUDGE.

Plaintiffs filed this putative class action on behalf of themselves and other similarly situated individuals who drive for Defendant Uber Technologies, Inc. Plaintiffs claim that they are employees of Uber, as opposed to its independent contractors, and thus are eligible for various statutory protections for employees codified in the California Labor Code, such as a requirement that an employer pass on the entire amount of any gratuity "that is paid, given to, or left for an employee by a patron.

* * *

I.   BACKGROUND

In a nutshell, Uber provides a service whereby individuals in need of vehicular transportation can log in to the Uber software application on their smartphone, request a ride, be paired via the Uber application with an available driver, be picked up by the available driver, and ultimately be driven to their final destination. Uber receives a credit card payment from the rider at the end of the ride, a significant portion of which it then remits to the driver who transported the passenger.

* * *

Before becoming "partners" with Uber, Plaintiffs and other aspiring drivers must first complete Uber's application process. Applicants are required to upload their driver's license information, as well as information about their vehicle's registration and insurance. Applicants must also pass a background check conducted by a third party. Would-be drivers are further required to pass a "city knowledge test" and attend an interview with an Uber employee. Interviewees are instructed to "[b]ring your car, dress professionally and be prepared to stay for 1 hour."

Once a prospective driver successfully completes the application and interview stages, the driver must sign contracts with Uber or one of Uber's subsidiaries (Raiser LLC). Those contracts explicitly provide that the relationship between the transportation providers and Uber/Raiser "is solely that of independent contracting parties." The parties "expressly agree that this Agreement is not an employment agreement or employment relationship." The relevant contracts further provide that drivers will be paid a "fee" (i.e., fare) upon the successful completion of each ride. According to an Uber 30(b)(6) deponent, Uber sets fares based principally on the miles traveled by the rider and the duration of the ride. Because Uber receives the rider's payment of the entire fare, the relevant contracts provide that Uber will automatically deduct its own "fee per ride" from the fare before it remits the remainder to the driver. Plaintiffs presented evidence that Uber typically takes roughly 20 percent of the total fare billed to a rider as its "fee per ride."

In this litigation, Uber bills itself as a "technology company," not a "transportation company," and describes the software it provides as a "lead generation platform" that can be used to connect "businesses that provide transportation" with passengers who desire rides. Uber notes that it owns no vehicles, and contends that it employs no drivers. Rather, Uber partners with alleged independent contractors that it frequently refers to as "transportation providers."

Plaintiffs characterize Uber's business (and their relationship with Uber) differently. They note that while Uber now disclaims that it is a "transportation company," Uber has previously referred to itself as an "On-Demand Car Service," and goes by the tagline "Everyone's Private Driver." Indeed, in commenting on Uber's planned expansion into overseas markets, its CEO wrote on Uber's official blog: "We are 'Everyone's Private Driver.' We are Uber and we're rolling out a transportation system in a city near you." Other Uber documents state that "Uber provides the best transportation service in San Francisco. . . ."

Moreover, Uber does not sell its software in the manner of a typical distributor. Rather, Uber is deeply involved in marketing its transportation services, qualifying and selecting drivers, regulating and monitoring their performance, disciplining (or terminating) those who fail to meet standards, and setting prices.

In addition to contending it is a technology company and not a transportation company, Uber argues the drivers are not its employees but instead are independent contractors, and therefore not entitled to the protection of the California Labor Code as asserted herein. In this regard, Uber contends it exercises minimal control over how its transportation providers actually provide transportation services to Uber customers, an important factor in determining whether drivers are independent contractors. Among other things, Uber notes that drivers set their own hours and work schedules, provide their own vehicles, and are subject to little direct supervision. Plaintiffs vigorously dispute these contentions, and claim that Uber exercises considerable control and supervision over both the methods and means of its drivers' provision of transportation services, and that under the applicable legal standard they are employees.

* * *

2. California's Test of Employment

The parties agree that determining whether Plaintiffs are employees or independent contractors is an analysis that proceeds in two stages. "First, under California law, once a plaintiff comes forward with evidence that he provided services for an employer, the employee has established a prima facie case that the relationship was one of employer/employee." "As the Supreme Court of California has held . . . the fact that one is performing work and labor for another is prima facie evidence of employment and such person is presumed to be a servant in the absence of evidence to the contrary." If the putative employee establishes a prima facie case (i.e., shows they provided services to the putative employer), the burden then shifts to the employer to prove, if it can, that the "presumed employee was an independent contractor."

For the purpose of determining whether an employer can rebut a prima facie showing of employment, the Supreme Court's seminal opinion in *Borello* "enumerated a number of indicia of an employment relationship." The "most significant consideration" is the putative employer's "right to control work details." S.G. Borello & Sons, Inc. v.

Dep't of Indus. Relations (Borello), 769 P.2d 399 (Cal. 1989). This right of control need not extend to every possible detail of the work. Rather, the relevant question is whether the entity retains "all necessary control" over the worker's performance.

The Supreme Court has further emphasized that the pertinent question is "not how much control a hirer exercises, but how much control the hirer retains the right to exercise." When evaluating the extent of that control, the Supreme Court has stressed that an employer's "right to discharge at will, without cause" is "strong evidence in support of an employment relationship." This is because the "power of the principal to terminate the services of the agent [without cause] gives him the means of controlling the agent's activities."

The putative employer's right to control work details is not the only relevant factor, however, and the control test cannot be "applied rigidly and in isolation." Thus, the Supreme Court has also embraced a number of "secondary indicia" that are relevant to the employee/independent contractor determination.

* * *

While the Supreme Court explained that all thirteen of the above "secondary indicia" are helpful in determining a hiree's employment status, it noted that "the individual factors cannot be applied mechanically as separate tests; they are intertwined and their weight depends on particular combinations." Moreover, the Court made it "clear that the label placed by the parties on their relationship is not dispositive, and subterfuges are not countenanced."

* * *

B.   The Plaintiffs Are Uber's Presumptive Employees Because They Provide a Service to Uber

If Plaintiffs can establish that they provide a service to Uber, then a rebuttable presumption arises that they are Uber's employees. Uber argues that the presumption of employment does not apply here because Plaintiffs provide it no service. The central premise of this argument is Uber's contention that it is not a "transportation company," but instead is a pure "technology company" that merely generates "leads" for its transportation providers through its software. Using this semantic framing, Uber argues that Plaintiffs are simply its customers who buy dispatches that may or may not result in actual rides. In fact, Uber notes that its terms of service with riders specifically state that Uber is under no obligation to actually provide riders with rides at all. Thus, Uber passes itself off as merely a technological intermediary between potential riders and potential drivers. This argument is fatally flawed in numerous respects.

First, Uber's self-definition as a mere "technology company" focuses exclusively on the mechanics of its platform (i.e., the use of internet enabled smartphones and software applications) rather than on the substance of what Uber actually does (i.e., enable customers to book and receive rides). This is an unduly narrow frame. Uber engineered a software method to connect drivers with passengers, but this is merely one instrumentality used in the context of its larger business. Uber does not simply sell software; it sells rides. Uber is no more a "technology company" than Yellow Cab is a "technology company" because it uses CB radios to dispatch taxi cabs, John Deere is a "technology company" because it uses computers and robots to manufacture lawn mowers, or Domino Sugar is a "technology company" because it uses modern irrigation techniques to grow its sugar cane. Indeed, very few (if any) firms are not technology companies if one focuses solely on how they create or distribute their products. If, however, the focus is on the substance of what the firm actually does (e.g., sells cab rides, lawn mowers, or sugar), it is clear that Uber is most certainly a transportation company, albeit a technologically sophisticated one. In fact, as noted above, Uber's own marketing bears this out, referring to Uber as "Everyone's Private Driver," and describing Uber as a "transportation system" and the "best transportation service in San Francisco."

Even more fundamentally, it is obvious drivers perform a service for Uber because Uber simply would not be a viable business entity without its drivers. Uber's revenues do not depend on the distribution of its software, but on the generation of rides by its drivers. As noted above, Uber bills its riders directly for the entire amount of the fare charged—a fare amount that is set by Uber without any input from the drivers. Uber then pays its drivers eighty percent of the fare it charges the rider, while keeping the remaining twenty percent of the fare as its own "service fee." Put simply, the contracts confirm that Uber only makes money if its drivers actually transport passengers.

Furthermore, Uber not only depends on drivers' provision of transportation services to obtain revenue, it exercises significant control over the amount of any revenue it earns: Uber sets the fares it charges riders unilaterally. The record also shows that Uber claims a "proprietary interest" in its riders, which further demonstrates that Uber acts as more than a mere passive intermediary between riders and drivers. For instance, Uber prohibits its drivers from answering rider queries about booking future rides outside the Uber app, or otherwise "soliciting" rides from Uber riders.

* * *

This Court holds, as a matter of law, that Uber's drivers render service to Uber, and thus are Uber's presumptive employees.

C.   *Whether a Hiree is an Employee or Independent Contractor is a Mixed Question of Law and Fact Generally to be Decided by the Jury*

Because the Court has determined that the Plaintiffs are Uber's presumptive employees, the burden now shifts to Uber to disprove an

employment relationship. As noted above, when determining under
California law whether a putative employer can rebut a hiree's prima
facie case of employment, the Court applies the multi-factor test laid out
in the Supreme Court's decision in *Borello*.

* * *

Put simply, the reasoning that juries should typically decide mixed
questions of law and fact supports the great weight of California
authority * * * that establishes that a hiree's status as either an
employee or independent contractor should typically be determined by a
jury, and not the judge.

*D.   Uber is Not Entitled to Summary Judgment Because Material
Facts Remain in Dispute and a Reasonable Inference of an Employment
Relationship May Be Drawn*

Because the ultimate determination of the Plaintiffs' employment
status presents a mixed question of law and fact, Uber may only obtain
summary judgment if all facts and evidentiary inferences material to the
employee/independent contractor determination are undisputed, and a
reasonable jury viewing those undisputed facts and inferences could
reach but one conclusion—that Uber's drivers are independent
contractors as a matter of law. The Court explained at the hearing on
this matter that this is a "pretty tough standard to meet," and it is one
that Uber has failed to meet here.

NOTES AND QUESTIONS

1.   In another case involving Uber in San Francisco, Mohamed v. Uber
Technologies, Inc., 848 F.3d 1201 (9th Cir. 2016), the Ninth Circuit reversed
Judge Chen and upheld a provision in Uber's software license agreement
with its drivers that all disputes are subject to arbitration.

2.   In McGillis v. Department of Economic Opportunity, 210 So.3d 220 (Fla.
Dist. Ct. App. 2017), an Uber driver was "deactivated" based on alleged
violations of Uber's privacy policy. When the driver filed for "reemployment
assistance" under Florida law his claim was rejected on the ground that he
was not an employee. In affirming the denial of his claim, the Florida
appellate court stated: "Due in large part to the transformative nature of the
internet and smartphones, Uber drivers like McGillis decide whether, when,
where, with whom, and how to provide rides using Uber's computer
programs. This level of free agency is incompatible with the control to which
a traditional employee is subject."

3.   Assuming that the court in *McGillis* is correct, that Uber drivers are not
employees under traditional common law criteria, should they be excluded
from unemployment insurance, workers' compensation, minimum wage and
maximum hour provisions, and all of the other laws designed to protect the
interests of workers? Do we need a new conceptualization of employment
laws to replace the New Deal era foundations of many labor and employment
laws?

4. On June 7, 2017, Secretary of Labor Alexander Acosta announced the immediate withdrawal of Labor Department interpretations from 2015 and 2016 involving independent contractors and joint employment. Of particular relevance is the guidance dealing with misclassification of employees as independent contractors, which contains a presumption that "most workers are employees." The Obama Administration had aggressively enforced the FLSA to obtain wages for workers, mostly low income, who were deemed independent contractors and therefore not subject to overtime provisions and other protections.

5. For a further discussion, see Miriam A. Cherry, Are Uber and Transportation Network Companies the Future of Transportation (Law) and Employment (Law)?, 4 Tex. A & M L. Rev. 173 (2017); Orly Lobel, The Law of the Platform, 101 Minn. L. Rev. 87 (2016); Benjamin Means & Joseph A. Seiner, Navigating the Uber Economy, 49 U.C. Davis L. Rev. 1511 (2016); Paul M. Secunda, Uber Retirement, 2017 U. Chi. L. Forum 435 (2017).

Dynamex Operations West, Inc. v. Superior Court
416 P.3d 1 (Cal. 2018).

■ CANTIL-SAKAUYE, C.J.

Under both California and federal law, the question whether an individual worker should properly be classified as an employee or, instead, as an independent contractor has considerable significance for workers, businesses, and the public generally. On the one hand, if a worker should properly be classified as an employee, the hiring business bears the responsibility of paying federal Social Security and payroll taxes, unemployment insurance taxes and state employment taxes, providing worker's compensation insurance, and, most relevant for the present case, complying with numerous state and federal statutes and regulations governing the wages, hours, and working conditions of employees. The worker then obtains the protection of the applicable labor laws and regulations. On the other hand, if a worker should properly be classified as an independent contractor, the business does not bear any of those costs or responsibilities, the worker obtains none of the numerous labor law benefits, and the public may be required under applicable laws to assume additional financial burdens with respect to such workers and their families.

Although in some circumstances classification as an independent contractor may be advantageous to workers as well as to businesses, the risk that workers who should be treated as employees may be improperly misclassified as independent contractors is significant in light of the potentially substantial economic incentives that a business may have in mischaracterizing some workers as independent contractors. Such incentives include the unfair competitive advantage the business may obtain over competitors that properly classify similar workers as employees and that thereby assume the fiscal and other responsibilities and burdens that an employer owes to its employees. In recent years, the relevant regulatory agencies of both the federal and state governments have declared that the misclassification of workers as independent contractors rather than employees is a very serious problem, depriving federal and state governments of billions of dollars in tax revenue and millions of workers of the labor law protections to which they are entitled.

The issue in this case relates to the resolution of the employee or independent contractor question in one specific context. Here we must decide what standard applies, under California law, in determining whether workers should be classified as employees or as independent contractors for purposes of California wage orders, which impose obligations relating to the minimum wages, maximum hours, and a limited number of very basic working conditions (such as minimally required meal and rest breaks) of California employees.

In the underlying lawsuit in this matter, two individual delivery drivers, suing on their own behalf and on behalf of a class of allegedly similarly situated drivers, filed a complaint against Dynamex Operations West, Inc. (Dynamex), a nationwide package and document delivery company, alleging that Dynamex had misclassified its delivery drivers as independent contractors rather than employees. The drivers claimed that Dynamex's alleged misclassification of its drivers as independent contractors led to Dynamex's violation of the provisions of Industrial Welfare Commission wage order No. 9, the applicable state wage order governing the transportation industry, as well as various sections of the Labor Code, and, as a result, that Dynamex had engaged in unfair and unlawful business practices under Business and Professions Code section 17200.

Prior to 2004, Dynamex classified as employees drivers who allegedly performed similar pickup and delivery work as the current drivers perform. In 2004, however, Dynamex adopted a new policy and contractual arrangement under which all drivers are considered independent contractors rather than employees. Dynamex maintains that, in light of the current contractual arrangement, the drivers are properly classified as independent contractors.

* * *

I.

* * *

Dynamex is a nationwide same-day courier and delivery service that operates a number of business centers in California. Dynamex offers on-demand, same-day pickup and delivery services to the public generally and also has a number of large business customers—including Office Depot and Home Depot—for whom it delivers purchased goods and picks up returns on a regular basis. Prior to 2004, Dynamex classified its California drivers as employees and compensated them pursuant to this state's wage and hour laws. In 2004, Dynamex converted all of its drivers to independent contractors after management concluded that such a conversion would generate economic savings for the company. Under the current policy, all drivers are treated as independent contractors and are required to provide their own vehicles and pay for all of their transportation expenses, including fuel, tolls, vehicle maintenance, and vehicle liability insurance, as well as all taxes and workers' compensation insurance.

Dynamex obtains its own customers and sets the rates to be charged to those customers for its delivery services. It also negotiates the amount to be paid to drivers on an individual basis. For drivers who are assigned to a dedicated fleet or scheduled route by Dynamex, drivers are paid either a flat fee or an amount based on a percentage of the delivery fee Dynamex receives from the customer. For those who deliver on-demand, drivers are generally paid either a percentage of the delivery fee paid by the customer on a per delivery basis or a flat fee basis per item delivered.

Drivers are generally free to set their own schedule but must notify Dynamex of the days they intend to work for Dynamex. Drivers performing on-demand work are required to obtain and pay for a Nextel cellular telephone through which the drivers maintain contact with Dynamex. On-demand drivers are assigned deliveries by Dynamex dispatchers at Dynamex's sole discretion; drivers have no guarantee of the number or type of deliveries they will be offered. Although drivers are not required to make all of the deliveries they are assigned, they must promptly notify Dynamex if they intend to reject an offered delivery so that Dynamex can quickly contact another driver; drivers are liable for any loss Dynamex incurs if they fail to do so. Drivers make pickups and deliveries using their own vehicles, but are generally expected to wear Dynamex shirts and badges when making deliveries for Dynamex, and, pursuant to Dynamex's agreement with some customers, drivers are sometimes required to attach Dynamex and/or the customer's decals to their vehicles when making deliveries for the customer. Drivers purchase Dynamex shirts and other Dynamex items with their own funds.

In the absence of any special arrangement between Dynamex and a customer, drivers are generally free to choose the sequence in which they will make deliveries and the routes they will take, but are required to complete all assigned deliveries on the day of assignment. If a customer requests, however, drivers must comply with a customer's requirements regarding delivery times and sequence of stops.

Drivers hired by Dynamex are permitted to hire other persons to make deliveries assigned by Dynamex. Further, when they are not making pickups or deliveries for Dynamex, drivers are permitted to make deliveries for another delivery company, including the driver's own personal delivery business. Drivers are prohibited, however, from diverting any delivery order received through or on behalf of Dynamex to a competitive delivery service.

Drivers are ordinarily hired for an indefinite period of time but Dynamex retains the authority to terminate its agreement with any driver without cause, on three days' notice. And, as noted, Dynamex reserves the right, throughout the contract period, to control the number and nature of deliveries that it offers to its on-demand drivers.

* * *

II.

We begin with a brief review of the relevant provisions of the wage order that applies to the transportation industry.

In describing its scope, the transportation wage order initially provides in subdivision 1: "This order shall apply to all persons employed in the transportation industry, whether paid on a time, piece rate, commission, or other basis," except for persons employed in administrative, executive, or professional capacities, who are exempt from most of the wage order's provisions.

Subdivision 2 of the order, which sets forth the definitions of terms as used in the order, contains the following relevant definitions:

"(D) 'Employ' means to engage, suffer, or permit to work.

"(E) 'Employee' means any person employed by an employer.

"(F) 'Employer' means any person as defined in Section 18 of the Labor Code, who directly or indirectly, or through an agent or any other person, employs or exercises control over the wages, hours, or working conditions of any person." (Cal. Code Regs., tit. 8, § 11090, subd. 2(D)–(F).)

Thereafter, the additional substantive provisions of the wage order that establish protections for workers or impose obligations on hiring entities relating to minimum wages, maximum hours, and specified basic working conditions (such as meal and rest breaks) are, by their terms, made applicable to "employees" or "employers."

Subdivision 2 of the wage order does not contain a definition of the term "independent contractor," and the wage order contains no other provision that otherwise specifically addresses the potential distinction between workers who are employees covered by the terms of the wage order and workers who are independent contractors who are not entitled to the protections afforded by the wage order.

III.

* * *

The difficulty that courts in all jurisdictions have experienced in devising an acceptable general test or standard that properly distinguishes employees from independent contractors is well documented. As the United States Supreme Court observed in [NLRB v. Hearst Publications] 322 U.S. 111, 121 (1944): "Few problems in the law have given greater variety of application and conflict in results than the cases arising in the borderland between what is clearly an employer-employee relationship and what is clearly one of independent, entrepreneurial dealing. This is true within the limited field of determining vicarious liability in tort. It becomes more so when the field is expanded to include all of the possible applications of the distinction."

As the above quotation suggests, at common law the problem of determining whether a worker should be classified as an employee or an independent contractor initially arose in the tort context—in deciding whether the hirer of the worker should be held vicariously liable for an injury that resulted from the worker's actions. In the vicarious liability context, the hirer's right to supervise and control the details of the worker's actions was reasonably viewed as crucial, because " '[ ]he extent to which the employer had a right to control [the details of the service] activities was . . . highly relevant to the question whether the employer ought to be legally liable for them . . . .' " For this reason, the question whether the hirer controlled the details of the worker's activities became the primary common law standard for determining whether a worker was considered to be an employee or an independent contractor.

* * *

In 1989, in [S.G. Borello & Sons v. Dep't of Indus. Rels.], 769 P.2d 399 [Cal. 1989] this court addressed the employee or independent contractor question in an opinion that has come to be viewed as the seminal California decision on this subject.

* * *

Crucially, the court in *Borello* then went on to explain further that "the concept of 'employment' embodied in the [workers' compensation act] is not inherently limited by common law principles. We have acknowledged that the Act's definition of the employment relationship must be construed with particular reference to the 'history and fundamental purposes' of the statute. [Citation.]" The court observed that "[ ]he common law and statutory purposes of the distinction between 'employees' and 'independent contractors' are substantially different" that "[f]ederal courts have long recognized that the distinction between tort policy and social-legislation policy justifies departures from common law principles when claims arise that one is excluded as an independent contractor from a statute protecting 'employees' ", and that "[a] number of state courts have agreed that in worker's compensation cases, the employee-independent contractor issue cannot be decided absent consideration of the remedial statutory purpose." The court in *Borello* agreed with this focus on statutory purpose: "[U]nder the Act, the 'control-of-work-details' test for determining whether the person rendering service to another is an 'employee' or an excluded 'independent contractor' must be applied with deference to the purposes of the protective legislation. The nature of the work, and the overall arrangement between the parties, must be examined to determine whether they come within the 'history and fundamental purposes' of the statute."

* * *

The adoption of the exceptionally broad suffer or permit to work standard in California wage orders finds its justification in the fundamental purposes and necessity of the minimum wage and maximum hour legislation in which the standard has traditionally been embodied. Wage and hour statutes and wage orders were adopted in recognition of the fact that individual workers generally possess less bargaining power than a hiring business and that workers' fundamental need to earn income for their families' survival may lead them to accept work for substandard wages or working conditions. The basic objective of wage and hour legislation and wage orders is to ensure that such workers are provided at least the minimal wages and working conditions that are necessary to enable them to obtain a subsistence standard of living and to protect the workers' health and welfare. These critically important objectives support a very broad definition of the workers who fall within the reach of the wage orders.

These fundamental obligations of the IWC's [Industrial Welfare Commission's] wage orders are, of course, primarily for the benefit of the workers themselves, intended to enable them to provide at least minimally for themselves and their families and to accord them a modicum of dignity and self-respect. At the same time, California's industry-wide wage orders are also clearly intended for the benefit of those law-abiding businesses that comply with the obligations imposed by the wage orders, ensuring that such responsible companies are not hurt by unfair competition from competitor businesses that utilize substandard employment practices. Finally, the minimum employment standards imposed by wage orders are also for the benefit of the public at large, because if the wage orders' obligations are not fulfilled the public will often be left to assume responsibility for the ill effects to workers and their families resulting from substandard wages or unhealthy and unsafe working conditions.

A multifactor standard—like the economic reality standard or the *Borello* standard—that calls for consideration of all potentially relevant factual distinctions in different employment arrangements on a case-by-case, totality-of-the-circumstances basis has its advantages. A number of state courts, administrative agencies and academic commentators have observed, however, that such a wide-ranging and flexible test for evaluating whether a worker should be considered an employee or an independent contractor has significant disadvantages, particularly when applied in the wage and hour context.

* * *

We find merit in the concerns noted above regarding the disadvantages, particularly in the wage and hour context, inherent in relying upon a multifactor, all the circumstances standard for distinguishing between employees and independent contractors. As a consequence, we conclude it is appropriate, and most consistent with the history and purpose of the suffer or permit to work standard in California's wage orders, to interpret that standard as: (1) placing the burden on the hiring entity to establish that the worker is an independent contractor who was not intended to be included within the wage order's coverage; and (2) requiring the hiring entity, in order to meet this burden, to establish each of the three factors embodied in the ABC test—namely (A) that the worker is free from the control and direction of the hiring entity in connection with the performance of the work, both under the contract for the performance of the work and in fact; and (B) that the worker performs work that is outside the usual course of the hiring entity's business; and (C) that the worker is customarily engaged in an independently established trade, occupation, or business of the same nature as the work performed.

* * *

In our view, this interpretation of the suffer or permit to work standard is faithful to its history and to the fundamental purpose of the wage orders and will provide greater clarity and consistency, and less opportunity for manipulation, than a test or standard that invariably requires the consideration and weighing of a significant number of disparate factors on a case-by-case basis.

* * *

IV.

* * *

We now turn to application of the suffer or permit to work standard in this case. As Dynamex points out, the trial court, in applying the suffer or permit to work definition in its class certification order, appears to have adopted a literal interpretation of the suffer or permit to work language that, if applied generally, could potentially encompass the type of traditional independent contractor—like an independent plumber or electrician—who could not reasonably have been viewed as the hiring business's employee. We agree with Dynamex that the trial court's view of the suffer or permit to work standard was too broad. For the reasons discussed below, however, we nonetheless conclude, for two independently sufficient reasons, that under a proper interpretation of the suffer or permit to work standard, the trial court's ultimate determination that there is a sufficient commonality of interest to support certification of the proposed class is correct and should be upheld.

First, with respect to part B of the ABC test, it is quite clear that there is a sufficient commonality of interest with regard to the question whether the work provided by the delivery drivers within the certified class is outside the usual course of the hiring entity's business to permit plaintiffs' claim of misclassification to be resolved on a class basis. In the present case, Dynamex's entire business is that of a delivery service.

Unlike other types of businesses in which the delivery of a product may or may not be viewed as within the usual course of the hiring company's business, here the hiring entity is a delivery company and the question whether the work performed by the delivery drivers within the certified class is outside the usual course of its business is clearly amenable to determination on a class basis. As a general matter, Dynamex obtains the customers for its deliveries, sets the rate that the customers will be charged, notifies the drivers where to pick up and deliver the packages, tracks the packages, and requires the drivers to utilize its tracking and recordkeeping system. As such, there is a sufficient commonality of interest regarding whether the work performed by the certified class of drivers who pick up and deliver packages and documents from and to Dynamex customers on an ongoing basis is outside the usual course of Dynamex's business to permit that question to be resolved on a class basis.

Because each part of the ABC test may be independently determinative of the employee or independent contractor question, our conclusion that there is a sufficient commonality of interest under part B of the ABC test is sufficient in itself to support the trial court's class certification order. Nonetheless, for guidance we go on to discuss whether there is a sufficient commonality of interest under part C of the ABC test to support class treatment of the relevant question under that part of the ABC test as well.

Second, with regard to part C of the ABC test, it is equally clear from the record that there is a sufficient commonality of interest as to whether the drivers in the certified class are customarily engaged in an independently established trade, occupation, or business to permit resolution of that issue on a class basis As discussed above, prior to 2004 Dynamex classified the drivers who picked up and delivered the packages and documents from Dynamex customers as employees rather than independent contractors. In 2004, Dynamex adopted a new business structure under which it required all of its drivers to enter into a contractual agreement that specified the driver's status as an independent contractor. Here the class of drivers certified by the trial court is limited to drivers who, during the relevant time periods, performed delivery services only for Dynamex. The class excludes drivers who performed delivery services for another delivery service or for the driver's own personal customers; the class also excludes drivers who had employees of their own. With respect to the class of included drivers, there is no indication in the record that there is a lack of commonality of interest regarding the question whether these drivers are customarily engaged in an independently established trade, occupation, or business. For this class of drivers, the pertinent question under part C of the ABC test is amenable to resolution on a class basis.

For the foregoing reasons, we conclude that under a proper understanding of the suffer or permit to work standard there is, as a matter of law, a sufficient commonality of interest within the certified class to permit the question whether such drivers are employees or independent contractors for purposes of the wage order to be litigated on a class basis. Accordingly, we conclude that with respect to the causes of action that are based on alleged violations of the obligations imposed by the wage order, the trial court did not abuse its discretion in certifying the class and in denying Dynamex's motion to decertify the class.

NOTES

1. See Ives Camargo's Case, 96 N.E.3d 673 (Mass. 2018) (newspaper delivery agent was an independent contractor and therefore not entitled to workers' compensation).

2. See generally Leo Buscaglia, Crafting a Legislative Solution to the Economic Harm of Employee Misclassification, 9 U.C. Davis Bus. L.J. 111(2008); Anna Deknatel & Lauren Hoff-Downing, ABC on the Books and in the Courts: An Analysis of Recent Independent Contractor and Misclassification Statutes, 18 U. Pa. J.L. & Soc. Change 53 (2015).

B. SOURCES OF MODERN EMPLOYMENT LAW

1. CIVIL SERVICE/PUBLIC EMPLOYMENT

Page 42. Please add the following note.

7A. In Borzilleri v. Mosby, 874 F.3d 187 (4th Cir. 2017), the plaintiff, an Assistant State's Attorney with nine years service, was discharged without cause four days after the newly-elected State's Attorney took office. The plaintiff alleged she was discharged because she had supported a rival candidate in the primary. Among other things, the plaintiff argued that because assistant prosecutors are officers of the court with distinct ethical obligations in prosecuting cases, the position does not involve policymaking. The Fourth Circuit rejected this argument and agreed with all the courts of appeals to consider the issue that assistant prosecutors have broad discretionary powers and therefore occupy policymaking positions. The Baltimore City State's Attorney's office at issue in the case employed over 100 prosecutors. Does this mean that upon election the new State's Attorney could discharge and replace all of them?

2. COLLECTIVE BARGAINING

Page 47. After the first paragraph, please insert the following.

In Janus v. AFSCME, 138 S.Ct. 2448 (2018), an Illinois public sector employer, whose employees were represented by AFSCME, charged all employees an agency (or "fair share") fee equal to about 78% of union dues for contract administration and other union expenses. The fee excluded union costs for lobbying and political activity. Nevertheless, the Supreme Court, five-to-four, in an opinion by Justice Alito, held that charging agency fees against unwilling employees amounted to a violation of the First Amendment. In so ruling, the Court overruled Abood v. Detroit Board of

Education, 431 U.S. 209 (1977). In dissent, Justice Kagan wrote that there was no justification for overruling established precedent that was workable and on which numerous public employers and employees relied.

Page 47. After the second paragraph, please add the following.

NOTE

The conservative shift in state legislatures has resulted in the enactment of more state right to work laws. As of 2017, there were right to work laws in 28 states, including the mid-western states of Indiana, Iowa, Michigan, Missouri, Nebraska, and Wisconsin. For a further discussion, see Raymond L. Hogler, The End of American Labor Unions: The Right-to-Work Movement and the Erosion of Collective Bargaining (2015).

5.   MODIFICATION OF THE AT WILL RULE

Page 55. Please insert the following case after Note 3.

Yardley v. Hospital Housekeeping Systems, LLC
470 S.W.3d 800 (Tenn. 2015).

■ SHARON G. LEE, CHIEF JUSTICE.

We accepted a question of law certified by the United States District Court for the Middle District of Tennessee to determine whether a job applicant has a cause of action under the Tennessee Workers' Compensation Act against a prospective employer for failure to hire if the prospective employer failed to hire the job applicant because that applicant had filed, or is likely to file, a workers' compensation claim against a previous employer, and if such a cause of action exists, what standard should apply. We hold that there is no cause of action for failure to hire under the Tennessee Workers' Compensation Act.

Factual and Procedural Background

Beginning in 1998, Kighwaunda M. Yardley worked as a housekeeping aide at the University Medical Center ("the Hospital") in Lebanon. In 2010, Ms. Yardley was hurt on the job and began receiving workers' compensation benefits. Between June 2010 and September 2012, she received medical treatment for her injury. As of July 1, 2012, she was performing light duty work for the Hospital's materials management group with the expectation that when released to full duty, she would return to her job as a housekeeping aide.

On January 1, 2012, the Hospital entered into a contract with Hospital Housekeeping Systems ("the Company"), whereby the Company agreed to provide housekeeping services for the Hospital beginning July 1, 2012. As part of its contract, the Company agreed to interview the Hospital's current housekeeping employees and, at the Company's discretion, hire the employees to continue in their positions. The Company hired most of the Hospital's housekeeping staff. As of July 1,

2012, Ms. Yardley had neither been interviewed nor hired because she was still on light duty. When Ms. Yardley was released to full duty, she sought to return to work in the housekeeping department. The Hospital referred her to the Company for employment. In August 2012, she spoke with the Company's Division Vice President, Michael Cox, who, according to Ms. Yardley, told her that the Company would not hire anyone receiving workers' compensation benefits. In an email to the Company, Mr. Cox said that Ms. Yardley had "been out on Workers['] Comp with the hospital long before [the Company's] arrival," that her shoulder was hurting her again, and that "[b]ringing her on board with [the Company] would seem to be a Workers['] Comp claim waiting to happen." Mr. Cox said he "would advise against [hiring Ms. Yardley] IF we have that option." After she was not hired, Ms. Yardley sued the Company in the United States District Court for the Middle District of Tennessee.

We accepted the following certified question of law from the federal district court: If a prospective employer refuses to hire a job applicant because that applicant had filed, or is likely to file, a workers' compensation claim incurred while working for a previous employer, can that applicant maintain a cause of action under the Workers' Compensation Act ("the Act") against the prospective employer for failure to hire, and if such a claim exists, should courts apply the motivating factor standard of causation, as they do with retaliatory discharge claims?

Analysis

* * *

This is a case of first impression. In Tennessee, there is no statutory or common law cause of action for retaliatory failure to hire. Ms. Yardley asks this Court to create this cause of action. Relying on public policy grounds and retaliatory discharge cases from this and other jurisdictions, Ms. Yardley argues that if employers can lawfully refuse to hire job applicants because applicants have filed, or are likely to file, workers' compensation claims, this action by employers will have a chilling effect on workers' decisions to file claims and obtain their rightful remedies under the Act. She also asserts that if employers are allowed to refuse to hire applicants on such a basis, it would frustrate the purpose of the Second Injury Fund, see Tenn. Code Ann. § 50–6–208 (2014), which the Legislature established to encourage the hiring of workers who have suffered previous injuries. Amicus curiae Tennessee Employment Lawyers Association argues that an employer's failure to hire a job applicant because the applicant asserted a claim for compensation against a previous employer constitutes a device that would relieve an employer of an obligation under the Act; such devices are prohibited by Tennessee Code Annotated section 50–6–114 (2014).

The Company and amicus curiae Tennessee Defense Lawyers Association oppose the creation of a cause of action for retaliatory failure to hire. They argue that there was no employer-employee relationship between Ms. Yardley and the Company and, therefore, the retaliatory discharge cases cited by Ms. Yardley are distinguishable. They contend that Tennessee's employment-at-will doctrine should be protected, that employers should be free to hire and fire as they choose, and that an exception to the employment-at-will doctrine should not be made in this case.

* * *

One exception to the employment-at-will doctrine is that an at-will employee may not be fired for taking an action encouraged by public policy. Filing a workers' compensation claim is an action encouraged by public policy. Therefore, an employer may not lawfully discharge an employee for filing a workers' compensation claim. An employee who believes that she has been fired for filing a workers' compensation claim may bring a claim for retaliatory discharge. This cause of action was recognized "to enforce the duty of the employer, to secure the rights of the employee[,] and to carry out the intention of the [L]egislature."

To decide whether a job applicant may bring a retaliatory failure to hire action against a prospective employer, we start by examining Tennessee Code Annotated section 50–6–114(a). When interpreting statutes, our primary function is to carry out the Legislature's intent without broadening the statute beyond its intended scope. To carry out this function, we presume that every word in a statute has meaning and purpose and should be given full effect, as long as the result does not violate the Legislature's obvious intent. When the statutory language is clear and unambiguous, we simply apply its plain meaning.

Tennessee Code Annotated section 50–6–114 provides, in part, "No contract or agreement, written or implied, or rule, regulation or other device, shall in any manner operate to relieve any employer . . . of any obligation created by this chapter. . . ." Although an employer's decision to fire an employee for filing a worker's compensation claim has been held to be an unlawful device, this holding does not apply to Ms. Yardley because she was not an employee of the Company. The Act applies to employers and employees. An employer is defined as "any individual, firm, association or corporation . . . using the services of not less than five (5) persons for pay." An employee is defined as a "person . . . in the service of an employer . . . under any contract of hire or apprenticeship, written or implied." Under this definition, Ms. Yardley was not an employee, but merely a job applicant. As such, the Company had no obligation to her under the Act.

Ms. Yardley argues that retaliatory discharge cases are analogous. The elements of a common law prima facie case for a workers' compensation retaliatory discharge claim are: (1) the plaintiff was an employee of the defendant at the time of the injury; (2) the plaintiff made a claim against the defendant for workers' compensation benefits; (3) the defendant terminated the plaintiff's employment; and (4) the claim for workers' compensation benefits was a substantial factor in the employer's motivation to terminate the employee's employment.

Ms. Yardley cites a number of retaliatory discharge cases to support her position and argues that the Tennessee and out-of-state cases cited form the basis for a retaliatory failure-to-hire cause of action. But these cases are distinguishable, as they all involve parties who had been in an employer-employee relationship with each other at the time the tort allegedly occurred. Ms. Yardley was not an employee of the Company, and thus, there was never a relationship. This is an important distinction. The employer-employee relationship involves mutual acquiescence, and certain levels of trust and dependence are created upon its formation. Both parties have rights and responsibilities that naturally flow from that relationship and which are not present before the relationship is formed. For this reason, failure to hire cannot be equated with termination of employment, as employees and job applicants are on different footing.

A few states have statutory provisions expressly allowing claims for retaliatory failure to hire. See, e.g., Fla. Stat. § 440.105(2)(a) 2 (2015); 775 Ill. Comp. Stat. Ann. 5/6–101 (2015); La. Rev. Stat. Ann. 23:1361 (2014); Me. Rev. Stat. tit. 5, § 4572 (2014); Mass. Gen. Laws Ann. ch. 152, § 75B (2015). Tennessee does not. We have found no judicial decision recognizing a claim for retaliatory failure to hire under state common law or public policy, and a number of courts have expressly refused to recognize such claims. See, e.g., Baker v. Campbell Cnty. Bd. of Educ., 180 S.W.3d 479, 484 (Ky. Ct. App. 2005) (holding that no cause of action exists under Kentucky public policy for retaliatory failure to hire); see also Peck v. Elyria Foundry Co., 347 Fed. Appx. 139, 148 (6th Cir. 2009) (declining to recognize failure-to-hire claims as a public policy exception to the employment-at-will doctrine under Ohio law); Sanchez v. Philip Morris, Inc., 992 F.2d 244, 249 (10th Cir. 1993) (declining to recognize common law failure-to-hire claims under Oklahoma law); Wordekemper v. W. Iowa Homes & Equip., Inc., 262 F. Supp.2d 973, 988 (N.D. Iowa 2003) (noting that "Iowa has never recognized a cause of action for retaliatory failure to hire or rehire a prospective employee based on that employee's past workers' compensation claims"); cf. Warnek v. ABB Combustion Eng'g Servs., Inc., 972 P.2d 453, 455–57 (Wash. 1999) (declining to recognize a common law claim for failure to rehire an employee on the basis of filing a workers' compensation claim, as "[t]here is a distinction between discharge . . . during the course of employment and not being rehired for new employment").

Ms. Yardley argues that if employers may legally refuse to hire job applicants because they have current or prospective workers' compensation claims, then employees will be discouraged from filing such claims. We find the alleged harm to be too speculative to justify an exception to the employment-at-will doctrine. This State has an interest in ensuring that its citizens have access to employment and the ability to earn a livelihood, but at the same time, employers should have freedom to choose their employees.

* * *

Conclusion

We respectfully decline to create an exception to the employment-at-will doctrine, and we therefore hold that a job applicant does not have a cause of action under the Tennessee Workers' Compensation Act against a prospective employer for failure to hire if the prospective employer refused to hire the job applicant because that applicant had filed, or is likely to file, a workers' compensation claim against a previous employer.

6. ARBITRATION

Page 55. Please delete the *Campbell* case and replace with the following.

Epic Systems Corp. v. Lewis
138 S.Ct. 1612 (2018).

■ JUSTICE GORSUCH delivered the opinion of the Court.

* * *

I.

The three cases before us differ in detail but not in substance. Take *Ernst & Young LLP v. Morris*. There Ernst & Young and one of its junior accountants, Stephen Morris, entered into an agreement providing that they would arbitrate any disputes that might arise between them. The agreement stated that the employee could choose the arbitration provider and that the arbitrator could "grant any relief that could be granted by . . . a court" in the relevant jurisdiction. The agreement also specified individualized arbitration, with claims "pertaining to different [e]mployees [to] be heard in separate proceedings."

After his employment ended, and despite having agreed to arbitrate claims against the firm, Mr. Morris sued Ernst & Young in federal court. He alleged that the firm had misclassified its junior accountants as professional employees and violated the federal Fair Labor Standards Act (FLSA) and California law by paying them salaries without overtime pay. Although the arbitration agreement provided for individualized proceedings, Mr. Morris sought to litigate the federal claim on behalf of a nationwide class under the FLSA's collective action provision, 29 U.S.C. § 216(b). He sought to pursue the state law claim as a class action under Federal Rule of Civil Procedure 23.

Ernst & Young replied with a motion to compel arbitration. The district court granted the request, but the Ninth Circuit reversed this judgment. The Ninth Circuit recognized that the Arbitration Act generally requires courts to enforce arbitration agreements as written. But the court reasoned that the statute's "saving clause," removes this obligation if an arbitration agreement violates some other federal law. And the court concluded that an agreement requiring individualized arbitration proceedings violates the NLRA by barring employees from engaging in the "concerted activit[y]," of pursuing claims as a class or collective action.

Judge Ikuta dissented. In her view, the Arbitration Act protected the arbitration agreement from judicial interference and nothing in the Act's saving clause suggested otherwise. Neither, she concluded, did the NLRA demand a different result. Rather, that statute focuses on protecting unionization and collective bargaining in the workplace, not on guaranteeing class or collective action procedures in disputes before judges or arbitrators.

Although the Arbitration Act and the NLRA have long coexisted— they date from 1925 and 1935, respectively—the suggestion they might conflict is something quite new. Until a couple of years ago, courts more or less agreed that arbitration agreements like those before us must be enforced according to their terms.

The National Labor Relations Board's general counsel expressed much the same view in 2010. Remarking that employees and employers "can benefit from the relative simplicity and informality of resolving claims before arbitrators," the general counsel opined that the validity of such agreements "does not involve consideration of the policies of the National Labor Relations Act."

But recently things have shifted. In 2012, the Board—for the first time in the 77 years since the NLRA's adoption—asserted that the NLRA effectively nullifies the Arbitration Act in cases like ours. D.R. Horton, Inc., 357 N.L.R.B. 2277. Initially, this agency decision received a cool reception in court. In the last two years, though, some circuits have either agreed with the Board's conclusion or thought themselves obliged to defer to it under Chevron U.S.A. Inc. v. Natural Resources Defense Council, Inc., 467 U.S. 837 (1984). More recently still, the disagreement has grown as the Executive has disavowed the Board's (most recent) position, and the Solicitor General and the Board have offered us battling briefs about the law's meaning. We granted certiorari to clear the confusion.

II.

We begin with the Arbitration Act and the question of its saving clause.

Congress adopted the Arbitration Act in 1925 in response to a perception that courts were unduly hostile to arbitration. No doubt there was much to that perception. Before 1925, English and American common law courts routinely refused to enforce agreements to arbitrate disputes. Scherk v. Alberto-Culver Co., 417 U.S. 506, 510, n. 4 (1974). But in Congress's judgment arbitration had more to offer than courts recognized—not least the promise of quicker, more informal, and often cheaper resolutions for everyone involved. So Congress directed courts to abandon their hostility and instead treat arbitration agreements as "valid, irrevocable, and enforceable." 9 U.S.C. § 2. The Act, this Court has said, establishes "a liberal federal policy favoring arbitration agreements." Moses H. Cone Memorial Hospital v. Mercury Constr. Corp., 460 U.S. 1, 24 (1983).

Not only did Congress require courts to respect and enforce agreements to arbitrate; it also specifically directed them to respect and enforce the parties' chosen arbitration procedures. Indeed, we have often observed that the Arbitration Act requires courts "rigorously" to "enforce arbitration agreements according to their terms, including terms that specify *with whom* the parties choose to arbitrate their disputes and *the rules* under which that arbitration will be conducted." American Express Co. v. Italian Colors Restaurant, 570 U.S. 228, 233 (2013).

On first blush, these emphatic directions would seem to resolve any argument under the Arbitration Act. The parties before us contracted for arbitration. They proceeded to specify the rules that would govern their arbitrations, indicating their intention to use individualized rather than class or collective action procedures. And this much the Arbitration Act seems to protect pretty absolutely. You might wonder if the balance Congress struck in 1925 between arbitration and litigation should be revisited in light of more contemporary developments. You might even ask if the Act was good policy when enacted. But all the same you might find it difficult to see how to avoid the statute's application.

Still, the employees suggest the Arbitration Act's saving clause creates an exception for cases like theirs. By its terms, the saving clause allows courts to refuse to enforce arbitration agreements "upon such grounds as exist at law or in equity for the revocation of any contract." § 2. That provision applies here, the employees tell us, because the NLRA renders their particular class and collective action waivers illegal. In their view, illegality under the NLRA is a "ground" that "exists at law . . . for the revocation" of their arbitration agreements, at least to the extent those agreements prohibit class or collective action proceedings.

The problem with this line of argument is fundamental. Put to the side the question whether the saving clause was designed to save not only state law defenses but also defenses allegedly arising from federal statutes. Put to the side the question of what it takes to qualify as a ground for "revocation" of a contract. Put to the side for the moment, too, even the question whether the NLRA actually renders class and collective action waivers illegal. Assuming (but not granting) the employees could satisfactorily answer all those questions, the saving clause still can't save their cause.

It can't because the saving clause recognizes only defenses that apply to "any" contract. In this way the clause establishes a sort of "equal-treatment" rule for arbitration contracts. The clause "permits agreements to arbitrate to be invalidated by 'generally applicable contract defenses, such as fraud, duress, or unconscionability.' " At the same time, the clause offers no refuge for "defenses that apply only to arbitration or that derive their meaning from the fact that an agreement to arbitrate is at issue." Under our precedent, this means the saving clause does not save defenses that target arbitration either by name or by more subtle methods, such as by "interfer[ing] with fundamental attributes of arbitration."

This is where the employees' argument stumbles. They don't suggest that their arbitration agreements were extracted, say, by an act of fraud or duress or in some other unconscionable way that would render any contract unenforceable. Instead, they object to their agreements precisely because they require individualized arbitration proceedings instead of class or collective ones. And by attacking (only) the individualized nature of the arbitration proceedings, the employees' argument seeks to interfere with one of arbitration's fundamental attributes.

* * *

III.

But that's not the end of it. Even if the Arbitration Act normally requires us to enforce arbitration agreements like theirs, the employees reply that the NLRA overrides that guidance in these cases and commands us to hold their agreements unlawful yet.

This argument faces a stout uphill climb. When confronted with two Acts of Congress allegedly touching on the same topic, this Court is not at "liberty to pick and choose among congressional enactments" and must instead strive " 'to give effect to both.' " A party seeking to suggest that two statutes cannot be harmonized, and that one displaces the other, bears the heavy burden of showing " 'a clearly expressed congressional intention' " that such a result should follow. The intention must be " 'clear and manifest.' " And in approaching a claimed conflict, we come armed with the "stron[g] presum[ption]" that repeals by implication are "disfavored" and that "Congress will specifically address" preexisting law when it wishes to suspend its normal operations in a later statute.

These rules exist for good reasons. Respect for Congress as drafter counsels against too easily finding irreconcilable conflicts in its work. More than that, respect for the separation of powers counsels restraint. Allowing judges to pick and choose between statutes risks transforming them from expounders of what the law is into policymakers choosing what the law should be. Our rules aiming for harmony over conflict in statutory interpretation grow from an appreciation that it's the job of Congress by legislation, not this Court by supposition, both to write the laws and to repeal them.

Seeking to demonstrate an irreconcilable statutory conflict even in light of these demanding standards, the employees point to Section 7 of the NLRA. That provision guarantees workers "the right to self-organization, to form, join, or assist labor organizations, to bargain collectively through representatives of their own choosing, and to engage in other concerted activities for the purpose of collective bargaining or other mutual aid or protection."

From this language, the employees ask us to infer a clear and manifest congressional command to displace the Arbitration Act and outlaw agreements like theirs.

But that much inference is more than this Court may make. Section 7 focuses on the right to organize unions and bargain collectively. It may permit unions to bargain to prohibit arbitration. But it does not express approval or disapproval of arbitration. It does not mention class or collective action procedures. It does not even hint at a wish to displace the Arbitration Act—let alone accomplish that much clearly and manifestly, as our precedents demand.

Neither should any of this come as a surprise. The notion that Section 7 confers a right to class or collective actions seems pretty unlikely when you recall that procedures like that were hardly known when the NLRA was adopted in 1935. Federal Rule of Civil Procedure 23 didn't create the modern class action until 1966; class arbitration didn't emerge until later still; and even the Fair Labor Standards Act's collective action provision postdated Section 7 by years. And while some forms of group litigation existed even in 1935, Section 7's failure to mention them only reinforces that the statute doesn't speak to such procedures.

A close look at the employees' best evidence of a potential conflict turns out to reveal no conflict at all. The employees direct our attention to the term "other concerted activities for the purpose of . . . other mutual aid or protection." This catchall term, they say, can be read to include class and collective legal actions. But the term appears at the end of a detailed list of activities speaking of "self-organization," "form[ing], join[ing], or assist [ing] labor organizations," and "bargain[ing] collectively." And where, as here, a more general term follows more specific terms in a list, the general term is usually understood to " 'embrace only objects similar in nature to those objects enumerated by the preceding specific words.' " All of which suggests that the term "other concerted activities" should, like the terms that precede it, serve to protect things employees "just do" for themselves in the course of exercising their right to free association in the workplace, rather than "the highly regulated, courtroom-bound 'activities' of class and joint litigation." None of the preceding and more specific terms speaks to the procedures judges or arbitrators must apply in disputes that leave the workplace and enter the courtroom or arbitral forum, and there is no textually sound reason to suppose the final catchall term should bear such a radically different object than all its predecessors.

The NLRA's broader structure underscores the point. After speaking of various "concerted activities" in Section 7, Congress proceeded to establish a regulatory regime applicable to each of them. The NLRA provides rules for the recognition of exclusive bargaining representatives, explains employees' and employers' obligation to bargain collectively, § 158(d), and conscribes certain labor organization practices. The NLRA also touches on other concerted activities closely related to organization and collective bargaining, such as picketing. It even sets rules for adjudicatory proceedings under the NLRA itself. Many of these provisions were part of the original NLRA in 1935, while others were added later. But missing entirely from this careful regime is any hint about what rules should govern the adjudication of class or collective actions in court or arbitration. Without some comparably specific guidance, it's not at all obvious what procedures Section 7 might protect. Would opt-out class action procedures suffice? Or would opt-in procedures be necessary? What notice might be owed to absent class members? What standards would govern class certification? Should the same rules always apply or should they vary based on the nature of the suit? Nothing in the NLRA even whispers to us on any of these essential questions. And it is hard to fathom why Congress would take such care to regulate all the other matters mentioned in Section 7 yet remain mute about this matter alone—unless, of course, Section 7 doesn't speak to class and collective action procedures in the first place.

* * *

IV.

* * *

The policy may be debatable but the law is clear: Congress has instructed that arbitration agreements like those before us must be enforced as written. While Congress is of course always free to amend this judgment, we see nothing suggesting it did so in the NLRA—much less that it manifested a clear intention to displace the Arbitration Act. Because we can easily read Congress's statutes to work in harmony, that is where our duty lies.

So ordered.

■ JUSTICE THOMAS, concurring.

* * *

■ JUSTICE GINSBURG, with whom JUSTICE BREYER, JUSTICE SOTOMAYOR, and JUSTICE KAGAN join, dissenting.

The employees in these cases complain that their employers have underpaid them in violation of the wage and hours prescriptions of the Fair Labor Standards Act of 1938 (FLSA), 29 U.S.C. § 201 et seq., and analogous state laws. Individually, their claims are small, scarcely of a size warranting the expense of seeking redress alone. But by joining together with others similarly circumstanced, employees can gain effective redress for wage underpayment commonly experienced. To block such concerted action, their employers required them to sign, as a condition of employment, arbitration agreements banning collective judicial and arbitral proceedings of any kind. The question presented: Does the Federal Arbitration Act (Arbitration Act or FAA), 9 U.S.C. § 1 et seq., permit employers to insist that their employees, whenever seeking redress for commonly experienced wage loss, go it alone, never mind the right secured to employees by the National Labor Relations Act (NLRA), 29 U.S.C. § 151 et seq., "to engage in . . . concerted activities" for their "mutual aid or protection"? The answer should be a resounding "No."

In the NLRA and its forerunner, the Norris-LaGuardia Act (NLGA), 29 U.S.C. § 101 *et seq.*, Congress acted on an acute awareness: For workers striving to gain from their employers decent terms and conditions of employment, there is strength in numbers. A single employee, Congress understood, is disarmed in dealing with an employer. The Court today subordinates employee-protective labor legislation to the Arbitration Act. In so doing, the Court forgets the labor market imbalance that gave rise to the NLGA and the NLRA, and ignores the destructive consequences of diminishing the right of employees "to band together in confronting an employer." Congressional correction of the Court's elevation of the FAA over workers' rights to act in concert is urgently in order.

To explain why the Court's decision is egregiously wrong, I first refer to the extreme imbalance once prevalent in our Nation's workplaces, and Congress' aim in the NLGA and the NLRA to place employers and employees on a more equal footing. I then explain why the Arbitration Act, sensibly read, does not shrink the NLRA's protective sphere.

* * *

Despite the NLRA's prohibitions, the employers in the cases now before the Court required their employees to sign contracts stipulating to submission of wage and hours claims to binding arbitration, and to do so only one-by-one. When employees subsequently filed wage and hours claims in federal court and sought to invoke the collective-litigation procedures provided for in the FLSA and Federal Rules of Civil Procedure, the employers moved to compel individual arbitration. The Arbitration Act, in their view, requires courts to enforce their take-it-or-leave-it arbitration agreements as written, including the collective-litigation abstinence demanded therein.

In resisting enforcement of the group-action foreclosures, the employees involved in this litigation do not urge that they must have access to a judicial forum. They argue only that the NLRA prohibits their employers from denying them the right to pursue work-related claims in concert in any forum. If they may be stopped by employer-dictated terms from pursuing collective procedures in court, they maintain, they must at least have access to similar procedures in an arbitral forum.

* * *

Recognizing employees' right to engage in collective employment litigation and shielding that right from employer blockage are firmly rooted in the NLRA's design. Congress expressed its intent, when it enacted the NLRA, to "protec[t] the exercise by workers of full freedom of association," thereby remedying "[t]he inequality of bargaining power" workers faced. There can be no serious doubt that collective litigation is one way workers may associate with one another to improve their lot.

Since the Act's earliest days, the Board and federal courts have understood § 7's "concerted activities" clause to protect myriad ways in which employees may join together to advance their shared interests. For example, the Board and federal courts have affirmed that the Act shields employees from employer interference when they participate in concerted appeals to the media, legislative bodies, and government agencies. "The 74th Congress," this Court has noted, "knew well enough that labor's cause often is advanced on fronts other than collective bargaining and grievance settlement within the immediate employment context."

Crucially important here, for over 75 years, the Board has held that the NLRA safeguards employees from employer interference when they pursue joint, collective, and class suits related to the terms and conditions of their employment. For decades, federal courts have endorsed the Board's view, comprehending that "the filing of a labor related civil action by a group of employees is ordinarily a concerted activity protected by § 7." The Court pays scant heed to this longstanding line of decisions.

In face of the NLRA's text, history, purposes, and longstanding construction, the Court nevertheless concludes that collective proceedings do not fall within the scope of § 7. None of the Court's reasons for diminishing § 7 should carry the day.

* * *

Further attempting to sow doubt about § 7's scope, the Court asserts that class and collective procedures were "hardly known when the NLRA was adopted in 1935." In particular, the Court notes, the FLSA's collective-litigation procedure postdated § 7 "by years" and Rule 23 "didn't create the modern class action until 1966."

First, one may ask, is there any reason to suppose that Congress intended to protect employees' right to act in concert using only those procedures and forums available in 1935? Congress framed § 7 in broad terms, "entrust[ing]" the Board with "responsibility to adapt the Act to changing patterns of industrial life." With fidelity to Congress' aim, the Board and federal courts have recognized that the NLRA shields employees from employer interference when they, e.g., join together to file complaints with administrative agencies, even if those agencies did not exist in 1935.

Moreover, the Court paints an ahistorical picture. As Judge Wood, writing for the Seventh Circuit, cogently explained, the FLSA's collective-litigation procedure and the modern class action were "not written on a clean slate." By 1935, permissive joinder was scarcely uncommon in courts of equity. Nor were representative and class suits novelties. Indeed, their origins trace back to medieval times. And beyond question, "[c]lass suits long have been a part of American jurisprudence." Early instances of joint proceedings include cases in which employees allied to sue an employer. It takes no imagination, then, to comprehend that Congress, when it enacted the NLRA, likely meant to protect employees' joining together to engage in collective litigation.

Because I would hold that employees' § 7 rights include the right to pursue collective litigation regarding their wages and hours, I would further hold that the employer-dictated collective-litigation stoppers, i.e., "waivers," are unlawful. As earlier recounted, § 8(a)(1) makes it an "unfair labor practice" for an employer to "interfere with, restrain, or coerce" employees in the exercise of their § 7 rights. Beyond genuine dispute, an employer "interfere[s] with" and "restrain[s]" employees in the exercise of their § 7 rights by mandating that they prospectively renounce those rights in individual employment agreements. The law could hardly be otherwise: Employees' rights to band together to meet their employers' superior strength would be worth precious little if employers could condition employment on workers signing away those rights. Properly assessed, then, the "waivers" rank as unfair labor practices outlawed by the NLRA, and therefore unenforceable in court.

II.

* * *

The FAA's legislative history also shows that Congress did not intend the statute to apply to arbitration provisions in employment contracts. In brief, when the legislation was introduced, organized labor voiced concern. Herbert Hoover, then Secretary of Commerce, suggested that if there were "objection[s]" to including "workers' contracts in the law's scheme," Congress could amend the legislation to say: "but nothing herein contained shall apply to contracts of employment of seamen, railroad employees, or any other class of workers engaged in interstate or foreign commerce." Congress adopted Secretary Hoover's suggestion virtually verbatim in § 1 of the Act, and labor expressed no further opposition.

Congress, it bears repetition, envisioned application of the Arbitration Act to voluntary, negotiated agreements. Congress never endorsed a policy favoring arbitration where one party sets the terms of an agreement while the other is left to "take it or leave it."

In recent decades, this Court has veered away from Congress' intent simply to afford merchants a speedy and economical means of resolving commercial disputes. In 1983, the Court declared, for the first time in the FAA's then 58-year history, that the FAA evinces a "liberal federal policy favoring arbitration." Soon thereafter, the Court ruled, in a series of cases, that the FAA requires enforcement of agreements to arbitrate not only contract claims, but statutory claims as well. Further, in 1991, the Court concluded in Gilmer v. Interstate/Johnson Lane Corp., 500 U.S. 20, 23 (1991), that the FAA requires enforcement of agreements to arbitrate claims arising under the Age Discrimination in Employment Act of 1967, a workplace antidiscrimination statute. Then, in 2001, the Court ruled in Circuit City Stores, Inc. v. Adams, 532 U.S. 105, 109 (2001), that the Arbitration Act's exemption for employment contracts should be construed narrowly, to exclude from the Act's scope only transportation workers' contracts.

Employers have availed themselves of the opportunity opened by court decisions expansively interpreting the Arbitration Act. Few employers imposed arbitration agreements on their employees in the early 1990's. After *Gilmer* and *Circuit City*, however, employers' exaction of arbitration clauses in employment contracts grew steadily. Moreover, in response to subsequent decisions addressing class arbitration, employers have increasingly included in their arbitration agreements express group-action waivers. It is, therefore, this Court's exorbitant application of the FAA—stretching it far beyond contractual disputes between merchants—that led the NLRB to confront, for the first time in 2012, the precise question whether employers can use arbitration agreements to insulate themselves from collective employment litigation.

* * *

III.

The inevitable result of today's decision will be the underenforcement of federal and state statutes designed to advance the well-being of vulnerable workers.

The probable impact on wage and hours claims of the kind asserted in the cases now before the Court is all too evident. Violations of minimum-wage and overtime laws are widespread. One study estimated that in Chicago, Los Angeles, and New York City alone, low-wage workers lose nearly $3 billion in legally owed wages each year. The U.S. Department of Labor, state labor departments, and state attorneys general can uncover and obtain recoveries for some violations. Because of their limited resources, however, government agencies must rely on private parties to take a lead role in enforcing wage and hours laws.

If employers can stave off collective employment litigation aimed at obtaining redress for wage and hours infractions, the enforcement gap is almost certain to widen. Expenses entailed in mounting individual claims will often far outweigh potential recoveries.

QUESTION

The majority and dissent disagree on the "agreement" to arbitrate all disputes in individual proceedings. The majority views this as a contractual term agreed to by both the employer and the employee. The dissent, however, considers it coerced, a product of a "take it or leave it" offer of employment. To what degree should the outcome of the case depend on how the agreement is viewed?

PART II

ESTABLISHING THE EMPLOYMENT RELATIONSHIP

CHAPTER 3

THE HIRING PROCESS

A. THE LABOR POOL

3. ALIENS UNAUTHORIZED TO WORK IN THE U.S.

Page 81. Please add the following at the end of the last paragraph on the page.

The number of unauthorized aliens in the U.S., 11 million, is roughly the same as it was in 2011. Jens Manuel Krogstad, Jeffrey S. Passel and D'Vera Cohn, Five Facts About Illegal Immigration in the US, Pew Research Center, April 27, 2017, available at http://www.pewresearch. org/fact-tank/2017/04/27/5-facts-about-illegal-immigration-in-the-u-s/.

Page 98. Note 5. Please add the following at the end of the note.

In EEOC v. Phase 2 Investments, Inc., No. JKB-17-2463, 2018 WL 1851480 (D. Md. Apr. 17, 2018), the district court read *Egbuna* narrowly as precluding unauthorized workers from bringing Title VII claims based on failure to hire, but not other types of Title VII claims. The court observed that in failure to hire claims, plaintiffs must show that they were qualified for the position, and that they necessarily cannot meet this requirement when they are not authorized to work. However, other types of Title VII claims, such as hostile work environment claims, do not require plaintiffs to show they were qualified for the position as part of their prima facie case.

Page 99. Note 10. Please add the following after the Wyoming statute in line 2.

But see In re Arellano, 344 P.3d 249 (Wyo. 2015) (upholding workers' compensation benefits; amendment to workers' compensation statute was interpreted to cover undocumented workers whom employers reasonably believed were authorized to work in the U.S. because the purpose of the amendment was to preclude common law actions for damages filed by undocumented workers who sustained injuries on the job).

Page 99. Note 10. Please insert on line 6, after the Connecticut case.

See Hernandez v. U.S.D. 233, 390 P.3d 875 (Kan. 2017) (workers' compensation award upheld for claimant who was not legally authorized to work in the United States and who used false name and documents to apply for job).

Page 100. Please add the following note.

14. More aggressive enforcement of immigration laws under the Trump Administration has resulted in a significant drop in workers' compensation claims filed in California by undocumented workers. What are the likely consequences for these workers, their employers, and workers authorized to work in the United States?

B. APPLICATIONS, INTERVIEWS, AND REFERENCES

2. INTERVIEWS

Page 122. Please add the following note.

7. Cities including Philadelphia and New York City have adopted laws banning employers from asking about applicants' salary histories. The purpose of these laws is to prevent an employee's new employer from replicating past pay discrimination, and instead determine salary based on qualifications. However, the Philadelphia Chamber of Commerce filed a lawsuit challenging the Philadelphia law as a violation of its members' First Amendment rights. A district court then enjoined the law, concluding that the City had failed to show that the law directly advanced the City's substantial interest, as required under the third prong of the test announced in Central Hudson Gas & Elec. Corp. v. Pub. Serv. Comm'n of NY, 447 U.S. 557 (1980). Chamber of Commerce of Greater Philadelphia v. Philadelphia, 2:17-cv-01548, 2018 WL 2010592 (E.D. Pa. Apr. 30, 2018).

3. REFERENCES

Page 129. Note 8. Please add the following to the end of the second paragraph.

In Syed v. M-I, the Ninth Circuit held that an employer failed to comply with the FRCA's disclosure requirement, which mandates a document that "consists solely of the disclosure," when it printed a liability waiver on the same page. 853 F.3d 492 (9th Cir. 2017).

Page 130. Note 10. Please add the following.

The most recent jurisdiction to reject compelled self-publication is Texas. Exxon Mobil Corp. v. Rincones, 2017 WL 2324710 (Tex. 2017).

Page 130. Please add the following after Note 11.

Pauline T. Kim & Erika Hanson, People Analytics and the Regulation of Information under the Fair Credit Reporting Act
61 St. Louis U.L.J. 17, 17–20 (2016).

People analytics—the use of big data and computer algorithms to make personnel decisions—has been drawing increasing public and scholarly scrutiny. Software is now available for screening applicants to identify the most promising candidates, or searching online profiles to find top prospects for recruitment. Algorithms claim to predict which workers will be most productive or which employees are most likely to leave their jobs. These tools are built by collecting and analyzing vast amounts of data about individual characteristics and behaviors that go far beyond traditional factors like education and training. The datasets are subject to data mining, a process by which computers examine the data to uncover statistical patterns. Those patterns are then used to make predictions about future cases and to inform decision-making.

As workplace use of data analytic tools expands, commenters are raising alarms about the potential unfairness of relying on them to make consequential employment decisions. Some concerns focus on the potential intrusiveness of the data gathering required to develop and use these tools. People analytics depend on the collection of large amounts of information, some of it highly personal. Efforts to harvest health-related data, or information about off-duty behavior and activities on social media potentially threaten employees' personal privacy. Even relatively trivial bits of information—when aggregated with other data about an individual—can reveal highly sensitive personal information. For example, information recorded by electronic activity trackers and collected as part of employee wellness programs can be analyzed to reveal when an employee is pregnant or trying to conceive.

Other commenters charge that people analytic tools can be unfair if the data contains errors or mischaracterizations. Inaccurate information in individuals' consumer records may cause them to unjustifiably lose out on employment opportunities. Employees have alleged that inaccuracies in reports about their criminal records or credit histories caused employers to deny them jobs. Similarly, when algorithms rely on error-ridden personal data, they may make inaccurate predictions that arbitrarily reduce individuals' employment opportunities. Even when personal information is technically accurate, it can be presented in ways that are misleading. And algorithms may draw inferences or make predictions that are unjustified, resulting in the arbitrary denial of employment opportunities.

In addition, big data tools may produce discriminatory effects. Although workforce analytics may sometimes help to counter biased human judgments, data is not always objective or neutral. Scholars have documented numerous ways that reliance on algorithms can result in discrimination. Relatively trivial information, such as zip code or Facebook "likes," may correlate closely with protected characteristics like race or gender, or reveal a person's political or religious views. These types of data may operate as proxies, allowing a biased employer to hide its discriminatory intent behind a seemingly neutral data model. Even when no discrimination is intended, algorithms can produce discriminatory outcomes. If, for example, the underlying data reflects biased judgments about workers' performance, an algorithm built using that data may simply reproduce that bias. In other cases, the data used to create the algorithm may not be representative of the workforce, resulting in a skewed model that systematically disadvantages groups of workers along the lines of race or other protected classification.

* * *

The FCRA establishes certain procedural requirements, and these can sometimes help individual workers challenge inaccurate information about them. However, although employers face significant liability risks if they disregard the statute's requirements, the FCRA in fact does little to curb invasive data collection practices or to address the risks of discriminatory algorithms. Examining how the FCRA does and does not apply to people analytics reveals the limitations of a purely procedural approach. Given these limits, protecting employee privacy and preventing workplace discrimination will require looking to other models of regulation.

D. MEDICAL SCREENING

1. PURPOSE

Page 147. Please delete the excerpt in D-1 and replace with the following.

Mark A. Rothstein, Jessica Roberts, and Tee L. Guidotti,
Limiting Occupational Medical Evaluations under the
Americans with Disabilities Act and the Genetic
Information Nondiscrimination Act
45 Am. J.L. & Med. 523, 525, 560–561, 565–566 (2015).

In the United States, occupational medical evaluations of applicants and employees began in the mid-nineteenth century. The use of medical criteria for selection and retention of employees was largely unregulated for over a century; employers and their physicians (either employees or consultants) had largely unfettered discretion in deciding what criteria to apply in making recommendations about individuals' fitness for various types of employment. The first regulation of occupational medical evaluations was incidental to legislation intended primarily to prevent discrimination in employment on the basis of disability (originally referred to as "handicap"). At the same time that workplace medical evaluations became subject to legal scrutiny, evolving professional norms of occupational medicine began limiting the scope of medical inquiry for fitness-for-duty and other evaluations.

* * *

Fitness-for-duty remains a central concern in occupational medicine and the most common area in which issues of the ADA—and less commonly, GINA—arise. Rather than assessing future risk of illness or disability, fitness-for-duty involves assessing present capacity to do the job as well as potential risk to self and others when performing work functions. Some employers attempted to control healthcare costs or reduce employee turnover by trying to identify future risk through medical screening. In the twentieth century, especially in the early decades, there had been a history of applying novel testing protocols to predict future disability, and tests were performed without proper scientific validation or with susceptibility to harm by chemical exposure. Sometimes this was the result of a new test being adopted before it was properly evaluated, and sometimes it resulted from the enthusiasm of management champions who seized on something they had heard about, but did not understand, as a way to reduce workers' compensation costs by excluding workers at risk. The result was that many workers who were entirely fit to do the work were unfairly disqualified from employment on the basis of tests of no value. Some of these tests, such as low-back X-rays (used to predict risk of low back pain but actually worthless), even carried some risk of harm, and few of them had any value or predictive accuracy. This is one reason that most tests currently used in routine occupational medical practice are simple and very old, such as the chest X-ray; another is that the limitations of the test are well known and results can be readily interpreted on the basis of vast experience, unlike a more sophisticated but novel test with which there is little experience.

* * *

In recent years, the conduct of occupational medical evaluations has been influenced by two independent but related factors: (1) the composition and practice standards of the occupational medicine workforce * * * and (2) increased legal regulation. * * * To begin with, it is clear that the practice of occupational medicine has evolved. Although the actual number of physicians practicing occupational medicine full or part-time has remained relatively stable for the last thirty years (at sub-optimal levels), the practice arrangements and conduct of medical evaluations have changed, There is little evidence on whether the actual practice patterns of physicians differ based on their employment arrangements, but occupational medical evaluations in all settings have changed in recent years to embrace more evidence-based medicine and more limited and targeted medical evaluations. Thus, controversial past practices, such as comprehensive medical questionnaires, single-sex "fetal protection" policies, and low-back X-ray practices, are no longer used. These modifications of occupational medicine practices may have taken place in any event, but they were certainly hastened by new developments in the law—both statutory and case law.

E. DRUG TESTING AND OTHER LABORATORY PROCEDURES

1. DRUG TESTING

Page 172. Please add the following to Note 11.

The Supreme Court of Colorado unanimously affirmed. Coats v. Dish Network, L.L.C., 350 P.3d 849 (Colo. 2015). The plaintiff challenged his firing under a Colorado law that prohibits discharge of an employee for engaging in "lawful activity" off the job (primarily designed to protect cigarette smokers). See p. 157, note 1. Would the plaintiff have had a better chance by alleging that permitting him to smoke marijuana at home for pain relief was a reasonable accommodation for his disability and therefore was required by the Americans with Disabilities Act or state disability nondiscrimination law? See Barbuto v. Advantage Sales and Marketing, 477 Mass. 456 (2017) (employee who used medical marijuana to manage Crohn's disease stated a claim of handicap discrimination under state law because off-site use of marijuana could be a permissible employment accommodation).

2. GENETIC DISCRIMINATION

b. LEGISLATIVE RESPONSES

(ii) Genetic Information Nondiscrimination Act (GINA)

Page 178. Please insert the following after the second paragraph.

The EEOC has issued amended regulations and interpretive guidance on employer sponsored wellness programs under GINA and the ADA. 81 Fed. Reg. 31126 (2016). However, a district court vacated the EEOC's rule allowing employers to offer incentives to encourage employees to participate in employer-sponsored wellness plans. Both the ADA and GINA permit employers to collect private health information as part of a "voluntary" wellness program, but neither statute defines voluntary. The court held that the EEOC did not adequately explain why it construed "voluntary" to allow employers to offer up to a 30 percent discount on employee health insurance contributions. AARP v. EEOC, 267 F.Supp. 3d 14 (D.D.C. 2017).

Page 178. Please delete the Poore case and replace with the following.

Lowe v. Atlas Logistics
102 F.Supp.3d 1360 (N.D. Ga. 2015).

■ AMY TOTENBERG, DISTRICT JUDGE.

Atlas Logistics Group Retail Services (Atlanta), LLC ("Atlas") operates warehouses for the storage of products sold at a variety of grocery stores. So one could imagine Atlas's frustration when a mystery employee began habitually defecating in one of its warehouses. To solve the mystery of the devious defecator, Atlas requested some of its employees, including Jack Lowe and Dennis Reynolds, to submit to a cheek swab. The cheek cell samples were then sent to a lab where a technician compared the cheek cell DNA to DNA from the offending fecal matter. Lowe and Dennis were not a match. With the culprit apparently still on the loose, Lowe and Dennis filed suit under the Genetic

Information Nondiscrimination Act ("GINA"), 42 U.S.C. § 2000ff et seq., which generally prohibits employers from requesting genetic information from its employees.

The matter is before the Court on the parties' Cross-Motions for Summary Judgment. The legal question before the Court is whether the information requested and obtained by Atlas was "genetic information" covered by GINA. For the reasons that follow, the Court concludes that it is. Thus, the Court GRANTS Plaintiffs' Motion for Partial Summary Judgment and DENIES Defendant's Motion for Summary Judgment.

* * *

III. Analysis

According to Plaintiffs Jack Lowe and Dennis Reynolds, the undisputed facts show that Atlas requested information about Speckin Labs's comparison of Lowe's and Reynolds's DNA to the fecal sample. These facts, Plaintiffs argue, demonstrate that Atlas violated 42 U.S.C. § 2000ff–1(b), which makes it "an unlawful employment practice for an employer to request, require, or purchase genetic information with respect to an employee." Plaintiffs therefore move for Partial Summary Judgment as to Atlas's liability under this section of GINA.

Atlas responds and argues in its Motion for Summary Judgment that the information the company requested concerning Lowe's and Reynolds's DNA analysis does not constitute "genetic information" as defined in GINA. According to Defendant's interpretation of GINA, "genetic information" refers only to information related to an individual's propensity for disease. For this reason, Defendant moves for summary judgment as to all of Plaintiffs' claims. The issue before the Court, therefore, is whether the term "genetic information" as used in GINA encompasses the information Atlas requested in this case.

* * *

A.   The Unambiguous Statutory Language of GINA

The Court begins its analysis with the language of GINA. GINA makes it "an unlawful employment practice for an employer to request, require, or purchase genetic information with respect to an employee. Section 2000ff–1(b) lists six exceptions to this general prohibition, but Atlas admits that none of the statutory exceptions apply here. The parties' disagreement centers on a single phrase in Section 2000ff–1(b): "genetic information."

GINA defines genetic information as "with respect to any individual, information about (i) such individual's genetic tests, (ii) the genetic tests of family members of such individual, and (iii) the manifestation of a disease or disorder in family members of such individual." 42 U.S.C. § 2000ff(4). Parts (ii) and (iii) do not apply to Lowe and Reynolds's claims, as the PowerPlex 21 analysis was not performed on DNA of their family members. Therefore, the DNA analysis would only qualify as "genetic information" under GINA if the analysis qualifies as a "genetic test."

"Genetic test" is also defined in GINA. The statute defines "genetic test" as "an analysis of human DNA, RNA, chromosomes, proteins, or metabolites, that detects genotypes, mutations, or chromosomal changes." 42 U.S.C. § 2000ff(7). The extent of GINA's guidance ends with its definition of "genetic test:" none of the words included in 42 U.S.C. § 2000ff(7) are further defined in GINA.

If all the Court considers is the language of GINA, the undisputed evidence in the record establishes that the DNA analysis at issue here clearly falls within the definition of "genetic test." The parties agree that Dr. Howenstine [of the testing laboratory] conducted an "analysis" of Lowe's and Reynolds's DNA. And the undisputed evidence in the record shows that this analysis at a minimum detects genotypes and mutations. Because the parties agree that Atlas requested a comparison of Lowe's and Reynolds's DNA to the fecal DNA found in the warehouse, Atlas's request and course of action appear to constitute a violation of 42 U.S.C. § 2000ff–1(b)'s prohibition against requesting genetic information from employees.

Defendant argues that this straightforward but broad interpretation of GINA is erroneous. Defendant urges the Court to interpret the "genetic test" language of GINA to exclude analyses of DNA, RNA, chromosomes, proteins, or metabolites if such analyses do not reveal an individual's propensity for disease. This proposed definition of "genetic tests"—a definition which limits genetic tests to those related to one's propensity for disease—renders other language in GINA superfluous, and should thus be rejected.

Section 2000ff–1(b) makes it unlawful to request, require, or purchase genetic information, except in six contexts. Section 1(b)(6), in turn, expressly allows employers to request, require, or purchase some genetic information which has nothing to do with the propensity for disease. Specifically, an employer is not liable under GINA where it conducts a "DNA analysis . . . for purposes of human remains identification, and requests or requires genetic information of such employer's employees, but only to the extent that such genetic information is used for analysis of DNA identification markers for quality control to detect sample contamination." 42 U.S.C. § 2000ff–1(b)(6). This exception would be unnecessary if Atlas's construction of GINA were correct, because under Atlas's construction, the term "genetic information" already excludes DNA analyses for purposes of human remains identification—a type of analysis unrelated to testing for disease propensity. Thus, the exception in § 2000ff–1(b)(6) weighs against Atlas's interpretation.

Atlas's reliance on GINA's legislative history to argue otherwise is unpersuasive. According to Atlas, this human remains identification exception was created to address a concern raised by the Bureau of

Alcohol, Tobacco, and Firearms ("ATF"). drafting of GINA, ATF expressed its concern that its DNA profile index, developed for forensic purposes, seemed to violate GINA as drafted. And Congress apparently carved out the narrow exception for law enforcement agencies in response to ATF's concerns. But Atlas does not explain why such an exception would be necessary if, as Atlas would have it, the definition of "genetic information" already excludes the type of information in ATF's index— genetic information unrelated to one's propensity for disease. The Court therefore rejects Atlas's interpretation, which is inconsistent with the plain terms of the statute.

* * *

IV. Conclusion

For the reasons discussed above, the Court finds Atlas liable under 42 U.S.C. § 2000ff and GRANTS Plaintiffs Jack Lowe and Dennis Reynolds Partial Motion for Summary Judgment as to liability. The Court DENIES Defendant Atlas Logistics Group Retail Services (Atlanta), LLC Motion for Summary Judgment as to all claims.

NOTE

Unlike all of the other discrimination laws enforced by the EEOC, since the effective date of GINA in 2010 until 2015 there were only 24 non-frivolous charges filed with the EEOC alleging violations of GINA, and 21 of them involved employer efforts to obtain or use family health histories. Only three cases alleged improper activity with regard to an employee's genetic information. Mark A. Rothstein, Jessica Roberts, & Tee L. Guidotti, Limiting Medical Evaluations under the Americans with Disabilities Act and the Genetic Information Nondiscrimination Act, 41 Am. J.L. & Med. 523, 554 (2015).

F. NEGLIGENT HIRING

Page 187. Please add the following to Note 4.

See also Roberto Concepcion, Jr., Need Not Apply: The Racial Disparate Impact of Pre-Employment Criminal Background Checks, 19 Geo. J. Poverty L. & Pol'y 231 (2012); Benjamin D. Geffen, The Collateral Consequences of Acquittal: Employment Discrimination on the Basis of Arrests without Convictions, 20 U. Pa. J.L. & Soc. Change 81 (2017).

Page 189. Please add the following to the end of Note 10.

Recent cases to uphold the potential liability of employers for negligent retention and supervision include Anicich v. Home Depot U.S.A., Inc., 852 F.3d 643 (7th Cir. 2017) (applying Illinois law, the court held that the employer's duty to monitor its employees extended to a supervisor's known harassing conduct that culminated in the employee's murder); Delorenzo v. HP Enterprise Services LLC, 207 F. Supp.3d 26 (D.D.C. 2016) (in cases based on fatal shooting of 7 employees at Washington Navy Yard by contractor's employee, all negligence actions were dismissed except for negligent retention and supervision).

CHAPTER 4

DISCRIMINATION

A. DISCRIMINATION ON THE BASIS OF RACE OR SEX

1. SOURCES OF PROTECTION

a. TITLE VII OF THE CIVIL RIGHTS ACT OF 1964

Page 194. Please add to end of subsection a.

The Act also established the Equal Employment Opportunity Commission (EEOC) and charged it with investigating charges of discrimination and enforcing federal antidiscrimination laws. As part of its mandate, the EEOC was required to engage in conciliation efforts with an employer in instances in which the EEOC determined that there was reasonable cause to believe that the charge was true. The adequacy of such pre-suit conciliation efforts has become its own source of litigation in EEOC initiated lawsuits. In Mach Mining, LLC v. EEOC, 135 S.Ct. 1645 (2015), the Supreme Court vacated a Seventh Circuit decision that shielded pre-suit conciliation efforts from judicial review. In *Mach*, the Supreme Court held that a court could review whether the EEOC had satisfied its conciliation obligation as a prerequisite to a Title VII action, but the scope of judicial review was narrow and the remedy for failing to conciliate was not dismissal, but a stay of the action and an order to the EEOC to conciliate. The Court then set forth the EEOC's pre-suit conciliation obligations in a two-part test. First, the EEOC "must inform the employer about the specific allegation." Second, the EEOC must try to engage the employer in an informal method of "conference, conciliation, and persuasion." Id. at 1652, 1656. On remand, the district court held that the EEOC had satisfied its conciliation obligations. EEOC v. Mach Mining, LLC, 161 F. Supp.3d 632 (S.D. Ill. 2016).

2. WHAT IS UNLAWFUL DISCRIMINATION?

a. DISPARATE TREATMENT

Page 217. Please insert at the end of the carryover paragraph from the prior page.

In Quigg v. Thomas Cnty. Sch. Dist., 814 F.3d 1227 (11th Cir. 2016), the Eleventh Circuit joined the Second, Third, Fourth, Fifth, Sixth, Seventh, Ninth, and Tenth Circuits in holding that at summary judgment, mixed motive claims involving circumstantial evidence should not be evaluated using the *McDonnell Douglas* standard. Instead, summary judgment should be denied in such cases if the plaintiff raises a genuine issue of material fact as to whether a protected characteristic was a motivating factor for the defendant's adverse employment action. Only the Eighth Circuit has continued to hold, post *Desert Palace*, that the *McDonnell Douglas* approach is appropriate at the summary judgment stage for mixed motive cases. See Griffin v. City of Des Moines, 387 F.3d 733 (8th Cir. 2004).

Page 234. Please add to the end of Note.

Moreover, in EEOC v. Bass Pro Outdoor World, L.L.C., 826 F.3d 791, 797–98 (5th Cir. 2016), the Fifth Circuit held that the EEOC was not required to meet the Rule 23 prerequisites of numerosity, commonality, typicality, and adequacy of representation when bringing an enforcement action in its own name because " '[w]hen the EEOC acts, albeit at the behest of and for the benefit of specific individuals, it acts also to vindicate the public interest in preventing employment discrimination.' "

(i) Harassment

Page 245. Please delete the last two sentences from the Note.

Page 252. Please insert as Note 5 and renumber subsequent notes accordingly.

5.   In Vance v. Ball State University, 133 S.Ct. 2434 (2013), the Supreme Court addressed the question of who is a "supervisor" for the purposes of a *Faragher*-type analysis. The Supreme Court explained that an employee is a "supervisor" under Title VII only if he or she is "empowered by the employer to take tangible employment actions against the victim." Id. at 2454. Following the Supreme Court's holding in *Vance*, the Sixth Circuit in Hylko v. Hemphill, 698 Fed. Appx. 298 (6th Cir. 2017), emphasized that "colloquial uses of 'supervisor' do not control the question of whether an employee is one," instead " '[s]upervisor' has various meanings in business settings, but has a specific meaning for the purposes of Title VII."

(ii) Because of Race

Page 258. Please add to the end of Note 2.

Trait mutability was also critical to the Eleventh Circuit's decision in EEOC v. Catastrophe Management Solutions, 852 F.3d 1018 (11th Cir. 2016). In *Catastrophe Management*, the Eleventh Circuit affirmed the district court's dismissal of plaintiff's disparate treatment claim of race discrimination challenging her employer's no dreadlocks policy. Title VII, the Eleventh Circuit held, prohibits only discrimination based on immutable traits.

Page 258. Please add as Note 5.

5.   In Village of Freeport v. Barella, 814 F.3d 594 (2d Cir. 2016), the Second Circuit did not take on the big question of what is race, but did hold that "Hispanic" is a "race" for the purposes of Title VII, and, more generally, that Title VII's definition of race encompasses ethnicity.

(iii) Because of Sex

(a) Sex Stereotyping

Page 264. Please add after first sentence to Note 2.

The Sixth Circuit relied on and affirmed its holding in *Smith* by holding in EEOC v. R.G & G.R. Harris Funeral Homes, Inc. 884 F.3d 560 (6th Cir. 2018) that discrimination against a transsexual employee for transitioning from male to female in her appearance at work was discrimination because of sex.

Page 264. Please delete the last paragraph on page 264 including the carryover text on page 265, and insert the following.

Recently there has been a great deal of attention to the question of whether Title VII's antidiscrimination mandate requires that transgender workers be permitted to use the bathroom associated with their gender rather than their biological sex. The EEOC has ruled that an employer violates Title VII if it denies a transgender employee access to the restroom corresponding to the employee's gender identity. See Lusardi v. Dep't of the Army, 2015 WL 1607756 (April 1, 2015). Federal courts have not yet followed the EEOC's lead. In Etsitty v. Utah Transit Auth., 502 F.3d 1215 (10th Cir. 2007), for example, a bus driver informed her employer that she was transgender and would begin to present as female at work and use female restrooms while on her route. Her employer terminated her because it was unable to accommodate her restroom needs. The Tenth Circuit held that Etsitty was not entitled to protection under Title VII because the employer's concern about potential liability stemming from her use of female restrooms, while still biologically male, was a legitimate business justification for burdening the plaintiff's gender expression. See also Kastle v. Maricopa County Commun. Coll. Dist., 325 Fed. Appx. 492 (9th Cir. 2009) (explaining that "after *Hopkins* and *Schwenk*, it is unlawful to discriminate against a transgender (or any other person) because he or she does not behave in accordance with an employer's expectations for men or women," but holding that the employer's ban on a transgender plaintiff's use of restroom for safety reasons did not constitute sex discrimination). Courts interpreting Title IX's prohibition on sex discrimination in the context of education have interpreted that statute to require that transgender students be permitted to use the bathroom associated with their gender identity. In G.G. ex rel. Grimm v. Gloucester Sch. Bd., 2016 WL 1567467 (4th Cir. 2016), for example, the Fourth Circuit held that the prohibition on sex discrimination under Title IX requires educational institutions to give transgender students restroom access consistent with their gender identity. In reaching its conclusion, the court relied heavily on guidances to this effect offered by the Obama Administration. In March 2017, the Supreme Court vacated and remanded the case to the Fourth Circuit because the Department of Education and Department of Justice under the Trump Administration had withdrawn the relevant guidances. See Gloucester Cty Sch. Bd v. GG, 137 S.Ct 1239 (2017). More recently, the Seventh Circuit in Whitaker v. Kenosha Unified Sch. Dist., 2017 WL 2331751 (7th Cir. 2017), held that a transgender student was likely to succeed on the merits of his Title IX claim alleging that his school's refusal to allow him to use the bathroom associated with his gender identity constituted sex discrimination. What may explain courts' reluctance to extend the sex stereotyping logic to cases involving individuals' choice of restroom? Is there any reason to interpret Title VII's antidiscrimination mandate differently from Title IX's in this regard?

Page 265. Please insert as new Note 4.

4. While most courts, as will be discussed at the end of the chapter, continue to hold that discrimination based on sexual orientation per se is not an actionable form of sex discrimination under Title VII, the Second Circuit in Christiansen v. Omnicom Group, Inc., 852 F.3d 195, 200–01 (2d. Cir. 2017), made clear that "gay, lesbian, and bisexual individuals do not have *less* protection under *Price Waterhouse* against traditional gender stereotype discrimination than do heterosexual individuals."

Page 271. Please insert at the end of Note 1.

The *Jespersen* opinion has not been free from criticism from other courts. In EEOC v. R.G. & G.R. Harris Funeral Homes, Inc., 201 F. Supp.3d 837, 853 (E.D. Mich. 2016), the court noted that it agreed with the dissent rather than the majority in *Jespersen* and held that an employer could not shield itself from liability under the sex stereotyping theory "simply by virtue of having put its gender-based stereotypes into a formal policy."

Page 271. Please insert the following at the beginning of Note 6.

6. As *Jespersen* makes clear, not all forms of sex-based differentiation violate Title VII. In Bauer v. Lynch, 812 F.3d 340, 351 (4th Cir. 2016), the Fourth Circuit held that an employer, in this case the Federal Bureau of Investigation, did not violate Title VII when it required male candidates seeking to become agents to complete 30 push-ups as part of their physical fitness test but required female candidates to complete only 14.

(b) Pregnancy

Page 272. Please insert the following case before Notes.

Young v. United Parcel Service, Inc.
135 S.Ct. 1338 (2015).

■ JUSTICE BREYER delivered the opinion of the Court.

The Pregnancy Discrimination Act makes clear that Title VII's prohibition against sex discrimination applies to discrimination based on pregnancy. It also says that employers must treat "women affected by pregnancy . . . the same for all employment-related purposes . . . as other persons not so affected but similar in their ability or inability to work." We must decide how this latter provision applies in the context of an employer's policy that accommodates many, but not all, workers with nonpregnancy-related disabilities.

* * *

We begin with a summary of the facts. The petitioner, Peggy Young, worked as a part-time driver for the respondent, United Parcel Service (UPS). Her responsibilities included pickup and delivery of packages that had arrived by air carrier the previous night. In 2006, after suffering several miscarriages, she became pregnant. Her doctor told her that she should not lift more than 20 pounds during the first 20 weeks of her pregnancy or more than 10 pounds thereafter. UPS required drivers like Young to be able to lift parcels weighing up to 70 pounds (and up to 150 pounds with assistance). UPS told Young she could not work while under a lifting restriction. Young consequently stayed home without pay during most of the time she was pregnant and eventually lost her employee medical coverage.

Young subsequently brought this federal lawsuit. We focus here on her claim that UPS acted unlawfully in refusing to accommodate her pregnancy-related lifting restriction. Young said that her co-workers were willing to help her with heavy packages. She also said that UPS accommodated other drivers who were "similar in their . . . inability to work." She accordingly concluded that UPS must accommodate her as well.

UPS responded that the "other persons" whom it had accommodated were (1) drivers who had become disabled on the job, (2) those who had lost their Department of Transportation (DOT) certifications, and (3) those who suffered from a disability covered by the Americans with Disabilities Act of 1990 (ADA). UPS said that, since Young did not fall within any of those categories, it had not discriminated against Young on the basis of pregnancy but had treated her just as it treated all "other" relevant "persons."

* * *

The District Court granted UPS' motion for summary judgment. It concluded that Young could not show intentional discrimination through direct evidence. Nor could she make out a prima facie case of discrimination under McDonnell Douglas. The court wrote that those with whom Young compared herself—those falling within the on-the-job, DOT, or ADA categories—were too different to qualify as "similarly situated comparator [s]." The court added that, in any event, UPS had offered a legitimate, nondiscriminatory reason for failing to accommodate pregnant women, and Young had not created a genuine issue of material fact as to whether that reason was pretextual.

On appeal, the Fourth Circuit affirmed. It wrote that "UPS has crafted a pregnancy-blind policy" that is "at least facially a 'neutral and legitimate business practice,' and not evidence of UPS's discriminatory animus toward pregnant workers." It also agreed with the District Court that Young could not show that "similarly-situated employees outside the protected class received more favorable treatment than Young." Specifically, it believed that Young was different from those workers who were "disabled under the ADA" (which then protected only those with permanent disabilities) because Young was "not disabled"; her lifting limitation was only "temporary and not a significant restriction on her ability to perform major life activities." Young was also different from those workers who had lost their DOT certifications because "no legal obstacle stands between her and her work" and because many with lost DOT certifications retained physical (i.e., lifting) capacity that Young lacked. And Young was different from those "injured on the job because, quite simply, her inability to work [did] not arise from an on-the-job injury." Rather, Young more closely resembled "an employee who injured his back while picking up his infant child or . . . an employee whose lifting limitation arose from her off-the-job work as a volunteer firefighter," neither of whom would have been eligible for accommodation under UPS' policies.

* * *

II

The parties disagree about the interpretation of the Pregnancy Discrimination Act's second clause. As we have said, * * * the Act's first clause specifies that discrimination " 'because of sex' " includes discrimination "because of . . . pregnancy." But the meaning of the second clause is less clear; it adds: "[W]omen affected by pregnancy, childbirth, or related medical conditions shall be treated the same for all employment-related purposes . . . as *other persons* not so affected but *similar in their ability or inability to work*." Does this clause mean that courts must compare workers only in respect to the work limitations that they suffer? Does it mean that courts must ignore all other similarities or differences between pregnant and nonpregnant workers? Or does it mean that courts, when deciding who the relevant "other persons" are, may consider other similarities and differences as well? If so, which ones?

* * *

The parties propose very different answers to this question. Young and the United States believe that the second clause of the Pregnancy Discrimination Act "requires an employer to provide the same accommodations to workplace disabilities caused by pregnancy that it provides to workplace disabilities that have other causes but have a similar effect on the ability to work." In other words, Young contends that the second clause means that whenever "an employer accommodates only a subset of workers with disabling conditions," a court should find a Title VII violation if "pregnant workers who are similar in the ability to work" do not "receive the same [accommodation] even if still other non-pregnant workers do not receive accommodations."

UPS takes an almost polar opposite view. It contends that the second clause does no more than define sex discrimination to include pregnancy discrimination. Under this view, courts would compare the accommodations an employer provides to pregnant women with the accommodations it provides to others within a facially neutral category (such as those with off-the-job injuries) to determine whether the employer has violated Title VII.

A

We cannot accept either of these interpretations. Young asks us to interpret the second clause broadly and, in her view, literally. As just noted, she argues that, as long as "an employer accommodates only a subset of workers with disabling conditions," "pregnant workers who are similar in the ability to work [must] receive the same treatment even if still other nonpregnant workers do not receive accommodations." She adds that, because the record here contains "evidence that pregnant and nonpregnant workers were not treated the same," that is the end of the matter, she must win; there is no need to refer to *McDonnell Douglas*.

The problem with Young's approach is that it proves too much. It seems to say that the statute grants pregnant workers a "most-favored-nation" status. As long as an employer provides one or two workers with an accommodation—say, those with particularly hazardous jobs, or those whose workplace presence is particularly needed, or those who have worked at the company for many years, or those who are over the age of 55—then it must provide similar accommodations to all pregnant workers (with comparable physical limitations), irrespective of the nature of their jobs, the employer's need to keep them working, their ages, or any other criteria.

* * *

We agree with UPS to this extent: We doubt that Congress intended to grant pregnant workers an unconditional most-favored-nation status. The language of the statute does not require that unqualified reading. The second clause, when referring to nonpregnant persons with similar disabilities, uses the open-ended term "other persons." It does not say that the employer must treat pregnant employees the "same" as "any other persons" (who are similar in their ability or inability to work), nor does it otherwise specify which other persons Congress had in mind.

* * *

III

The statute lends itself to an interpretation other than those that the parties advocate and that the dissent sets forth. Our interpretation minimizes the problems we have discussed, responds directly to *Gilbert*, and is consistent with longstanding interpretations of Title VII.

In our view, an individual pregnant worker who seeks to show disparate treatment through indirect evidence may do so through application of the *McDonnell Douglas* framework. That framework requires a plaintiff to make out a prima facie case of discrimination. But it is "not intended to be an inflexible rule." Furnco Constr. Corp. v. Waters, 438 U.S. 567, 575 (1978). Rather, an individual plaintiff may establish a prima facie case by "showing actions taken by the employer from which one can infer, if such actions remain unexplained, that it is more likely than not that such actions were based on a discriminatory criterion illegal under" Title VII. The burden of making this showing is "not onerous." In particular, making this showing is not as burdensome as succeeding on "an ultimate finding of fact as to" a discriminatory employment action. Neither does it require the plaintiff to show that those whom the employer favored and those whom the employer disfavored were similar in all but the protected ways.

Thus, a plaintiff alleging that the denial of an accommodation constituted disparate treatment under the Pregnancy Discrimination Act's second clause may make out a prima facie case by showing, as in *McDonnell Douglas*, that she belongs to the protected class, that she sought accommodation, that the employer did not accommodate her, and that the employer did accommodate others "similar in their ability or inability to work."

The employer may then seek to justify its refusal to accommodate the plaintiff by relying on "legitimate, nondiscriminatory" reasons for denying her accommodation. But, consistent with the Act's basic objective, that reason normally cannot consist simply of a claim that it is more expensive or less convenient to add pregnant women to the category of those ("similar in their ability or inability to work") whom the employer accommodates. After all, the employer in *Gilbert* could in all likelihood have made just such a claim.

If the employer offers an apparently "legitimate, non-discriminatory" reason for its actions, the plaintiff may in turn show that the employer's proffered reasons are in fact pretextual. We believe that the plaintiff may reach a jury on this issue by providing sufficient evidence that the employer's policies impose a significant burden on pregnant workers, and that the employer's "legitimate, nondiscriminatory" reasons are not sufficiently strong to justify the burden, but rather—when considered along with the burden imposed—give rise to an inference of intentional discrimination.

The plaintiff can create a genuine issue of material fact as to whether a significant burden exists by providing evidence that the employer accommodates a large percentage of nonpregnant workers while failing to accommodate a large percentage of pregnant workers. Here, for example, if the facts are as Young says they are, she can show that UPS accommodates most nonpregnant employees with lifting limitations while categorically failing to accommodate pregnant employees with lifting limitations. Young might also add that the fact that UPS has multiple policies that accommodate nonpregnant employees with lifting restrictions suggests that its reasons for failing to accommodate pregnant employees with lifting restrictions are not sufficiently strong—to the point that a jury could find that its reasons for failing to accommodate pregnant employees give rise to an inference of intentional discrimination.

* * *

IV

Under this interpretation of the Act, the judgment of the Fourth Circuit must be vacated. A party is entitled to summary judgment if there is "no genuine dispute as to any material fact and the movant is entitled to judgment as a matter of law." Fed. Rule Civ. Proc. 56(a). We have already outlined the evidence Young introduced. Viewing the record in the light most favorable to Young, there is a genuine dispute as to whether UPS provided more favorable treatment to at least some employees whose situation cannot reasonably be distinguished from Young's. In other words, Young created a genuine dispute of material fact as to the fourth prong of the *McDonnell Douglas* analysis.

* * *

We do not determine whether Young created a genuine issue of material fact as to whether UPS' reasons for having treated Young less favorably than it treated these other nonpregnant employees were pretextual. We leave a final determination of that question for the Fourth Circuit to make on remand, in light of the interpretation of the Pregnancy Discrimination Act that we have set out above.

* * *

For the reasons above, we vacate the judgment of the Fourth Circuit and remand the case for further proceedings consistent with this opinion.

It is so ordered.

Page 272. Please delete Note 2 and insert the following.

2.   In *Young*, the Supreme Court made clear that the PDA does not grant pregnant workers a "most-favored-nation status" entitling them to the very best treatment that the employer provides to another group of employees similar in their ability or inability to work. Nonetheless, the Court also explained that an employer cannot always protect itself from liability simply by pointing to some other group of workers similar in their ability or inability to work that it treats similarly to pregnant workers. Instead, a plaintiff may still win if she can convince a jury that there is no legitimate non-discriminatory reason for the employer's policies treating pregnant workers less favorably than other similarly situated categories of non-pregnant workers. For large employers who distinguish between many types of disabled workers, how much guidance does the Court's ruling in *Young* provide about which particular subset of employees pregnant women will be compared to and when an employer will be found in violation of Title VII? State law may provide pregnant workers with greater protection. In January 2014, New Jersey amended its Law Against Discrimination to not only explicitly prohibit discrimination against pregnant women but also to require employers to make reasonable accommodations available to pregnant workers. N.J.S.A. 10:5–12. However, should an employer choose to provide special accommodations to pregnant employees, it may not necessarily be able to force the employees to accept the accommodations. This is particularly relevant when accommodations involve a reduction in hours or responsibilities resulting in a lower salary. In EEOC v. Catholic Healthcare W., 530 F. Supp.2d 1096 (C.D. Cal. 2008), a federal district court applied the BFOQ test to Catholic Healthcare's unsolicited transfer of a pregnant radiology technologist to a different area of work. Catholic Healthcare's transfer was found to be discriminatory.

b.   DISPARATE IMPACT/ADVERSE IMPACT

Page 292. Please insert at the end of first full paragraph.

In Jones v. City of Boston, 845 F.3d 28, 31 (1st Cir. 2016) for example, the First Circuit deviated from the standard four-fifths rule of thumb to find an actionable disparate impact in a case involving a hair drug test that resulted in 99% of whites testing negative and 98% of blacks testing negative because "the difference in exam results by race was indisputably statistically significant."

B. PROCEDURE

1. FILING A CHARGE OF EMPLOYMENT DISCRIMINATION

Page 323. Please insert before first full paragraph.

Federal employees must file a charge with the EEOC within 45 days of the "date of the matter alleged to be discriminatory" in order to preserve the right to sue in federal court for a violation of Title VII. In Green v. Brennan, 136 S.Ct. 1769 (2016), the Supreme Court held that for an employee alleging "constructive discharge" in violation of Title VII, the statutory period begins to run only after the employee resigns, not, as some circuits had previously held, at the time of the employer's last allegedly discriminatory act giving rise to the resignation.

3. PROVING DISCRIMINATION

Page 330. Please insert at the end of note.

In Vasquez v. Empress Ambulance Service, 835 F.3d 267, 272–73 (2nd Cir. 2016), the Second Circuit held that "the 'cat's paw' theory may also be used to support recovery for claims of retaliation in violation of Title VII."

C. RETALIATION

Page 341. Please add to end of note.

The Court in *Nassar* was silent on how its ruling affected summary judgment standards, and a circuit split has emerged on the issue. Compare Foster v. University of Maryland-Eastern Shore, 787 F.3d 243 (4th Cir. 2015) (holding that *Nassar* did not change the plaintiff's burden of proof regarding the prima facie case and the need to present evidence of pretext in order to survive summary judgment on a retaliation claim brought under the *McDonnell Douglas* standard) with EEOC v. Ford Motor Co., 782 F.3d 753 (6th Cir. 2015) (requiring evidence of but for causation as part of plaintiff's prima facie case in order for plaintiff to survive summary judgment on her retaliation claim).

E. DISCRIMINATION BASED ON FACTORS OTHER THAN RACE OR SEX

1. RELIGION

Page 370. Please replace Note 16 with the following.

16. What must an employee do to trigger an employer's duty to accommodate her religion? In EEOC v. Abercrombie & Fitch, 135 S.Ct. 2028 (2015) (see also case excerpt in Chapter 7), the Supreme Court distinguished between motive and knowledge, making clear that a disparate treatment claim may succeed if an employer acts with the motive of avoiding accommodation even if the employer lacks actual knowledge that the applicant in fact needs a religious accommodation. In other words, an applicant need not provide explicit notification to a prospective employer that a particular practice is religiously motivated and would require accommodation in order to trigger the employer's duty to provide religious accommodation. An employer may be found liable if its motive is to avoid accommodation even if the employer is acting on no more than "an unsubstantiated suspicion" that religious accommodation would be needed. Consistent with the Court's ruling in *Abercrombie & Fitch*, is the earlier decision by the Seventh Circuit in Adeyeye v. Heartland Sweeteners, LLC, 721 F.3d 444 (7th Cir. 2013), in which the court held that an employee's request to take unpaid leave to attend the funeral ceremonies of his father in Nigeria was sufficient to put the employer on notice of the religious nature of the request. The court explained that even though the plaintiff's religious beliefs and practices were unfamiliar to most Americans, his request for leave gave sufficient notice of the religious nature of the leave by referring to "a funeral ceremony,' a 'funeral rite,' and animal sacrifice." Moreover, the court explained that "[i]f the managers who considered the request had questions about whether the request was religious, nothing would have prevented them from asking Adeyeye to explain a little more about the nature of his request. . . ."

Page 371. Please insert as new Note 19 and renumber subsequent notes accordingly.

19. In addition to the religious exemptions to Title VII found in Section 702, the Religious Freedom Restoration Act provides additional protection for employers. In Burwell v. Hobby Lobby, 134 S.Ct 2751, 2761 (2014) (p. 541 of the main volume), the Supreme Court held that persons or "closely held" companies were entitled to exemption under RFRA from neutral laws of general applicability that burdened the exercise of religion unless the government demonstrated that the application of the burden "1) is in furtherance of a compelling governmental interest; and 2) is the least restrictive means of furthering that compelling interest." Relying on *Hobby Lobby*, the court in EEOC v. R.G. & B.R. Harris Funeral Homes, 201 F. Supp.3d 837, 842 (E.D. Mich. 2016), held that a funeral home was entitled to a RFRA exemption from "Title VII, and the body of sex-stereotyping case law that has developed under it."

3. AGE

Page 393. Please insert in Note 4 after second full sentence. Please move the remainder of the note to create a new note 5 and renumber the rest of the notes accordingly.

There is disagreement, however, about whether the ADEA's requirement that employers have 20 or more employees also applies to state and local employers. In Guido v. Mount Lemmon Fire District, 859 F.3d 1168 (9th Cir. 2017), the Ninth Circuit held that there is no small employer exception for state and local employers and hence that the ADEA applies to all such employers regardless of size. The Sixth, Seventh, Eighth and Tenth Circuits have disagreed. The Supreme Court has recently granted cert. in Mount Lemmon Fire District v. Guido, 138 S.Ct. 1165 (2018).

Page 393. Please insert in new Note 6 after third full sentence and delete the rest of the note.

The ADEA may not, however, be the exclusive remedy for workers alleging age discrimination. In Levin v. Madigan, 692 F.3d 607 (7th Cir. 2012), the Seventh Circuit permitted a state employee to bring an equal protection claim for age discrimination under 42 U.S.C. § 1983. While several district courts have ruled similarly, the other circuit courts to consider the issue have held that the ADEA is the exclusive remedy for age discrimination claims. Compare Shapiro v. N.T. City Dep't of Educ., 561 F.Supp.2d 413 (S.D.N.Y. 2008) (ADEA does not preclude a § 1983 claim) and Mustafa v. State of Deb. Dep't of Corr. Servs., 196 F.Supp.2d 945 (D. Neb. 2002) (same) with Hildebrand v. Allegheny Cnty., 757 F.3d 99 (3d Cir. 2014) (holding that a state or local government employee may not maintain an age discrimination claim under § 1983, but must instead proceed under the ADEA); Zombro v. Baltimore City Police Dep't, 868 F.2d 1364 (4th Cir. 1989) (same); Ahlmeyer v. Nev. Sys. of Higher Ed., 555 F.3d 1051 (9th Cir. 2009) (same); Tapia-Tapia v. Potter, 322 F.3d 742 (1st Cir. 2003) (same); Lafleur v. Tex. Dep't of Health, 126 F.3d 758 (5th Cir. 1997) (same); Chennareddy v. Bowsher, 935 F.2d 315 (D.C. Cir. 191) (same). The Supreme Court accepted cert in Madigan v. Levin for the 2013 term, but then dismissed it as improvidently granted, 134 S.Ct. 2 (2013).

Page 395. Please insert at the beginning of new Note 10.

10. In Karlo v. Pittsburgh Glass Works, 849 F.3d 61 (3d Cir. 2017), the Third Circuit held that plaintiffs could show a disparate impact under the ADEA based on subgroup comparisons and were not limited to comparisons simply between employees age 40 and above and those under 40.

Page 395. Please insert at the end of new Note 11.

However, in Tramp v. Associated Underwriters, 768 F3d 793 (8th Cir. 2014), a disparate treatment case, the Eighth Circuit held that an employer's consideration of health care costs in making decisions about which employees to terminate could constitute age discrimination if the employer "supposes a correlation" between costs and age "and acts accordingly." Id. at 802.

Page 395. Please insert as Note 12 and renumber subsequent notes accordingly.

12. In 2016, the Eleventh Circuit vacated its prior decision in Villarreal v. R.J. Reynolds Tobacco Co, 806 F.3d 1288 (11th Cir. 2015), in which a panel of the Eleventh Circuit held that job seekers—not just employees—may bring disparate impact claims under the ADEA. Rehearing the case en banc, the Eleventh Circuit held that the text of the ADEA "makes clear that an applicant for employment cannot sue an employer for disparate impact because the applicant has no 'status as an employee.'" 839 F.3d 958 (11th Cir. 2016) (en banc). Recently, the Seventh Circuit reached the opposite conclusion in Kleber v. CareFusion Corp., 888 F.3d 868 (7th Cir. 2018), in which it held that job applicants are protected under the ADEA.

Page 397. Please insert at the end of new Note 17.

In a recently filed case, Communication Workers of America v. T-Mobile U.S. (N.D. Cal. 2017) (No. 5:17-cv-07232), the plaintiffs argue that the defendants, which includes hundreds of major American employers and employment agencies, violated the ADEA by excluding older workers from receiving their employment and recruiting ads on Facebook.

4. DISABILITY

Page 406. Please add to the end of Note 1.

However, in Blatt v. Cabela's Retail, Inc., No. 5:14-cv-04822-JFL (E.D. Pa., filed Aug. 15, 2014), a transgender plaintiff argued that the ADA's exclusion of gender identity disorders violates the Equal Protection Clause of the U.S. Constitution. On September 21, 2015, the district court ordered the Department of Justice to intervene or file a supplemental statement of interest regarding the constitutionality of the gender identity disorder exclusion in the ADA. Subsequently, the *Blatt* court held that it could avoid the constitutional issue if it interpreted the term "gender identity disorders" in the ADA "narrowly to refer to simply the condition of identifying with a different gender, not to exclude from ADA coverage disabling conditions that persons who identify with a different gender may have—such as Blatt's gender dysphoria, which substantially limits her major life activities of interacting with others, reproducing, and social and occupational functioning." Given this interpretation of the ADA, the court concluded that Blatt's gender dysphoria was not excluded from protection and denied the defendant's motion to dismiss. Blatt v. Cabela's Retail, Inc., 2017 WL 2178123 (E.D. Pa., May 18, 2017).

5. SEXUAL ORIENTATION

Page 417. Please delete entire section 5 and replace with the following.

Hively v. Ivy Tech Community College of Indiana
853 F.3d 339 (7th Cir. 2017) (en banc).

■ WOOD, CHIEF JUDGE.

Title VII of the Civil Rights Act of 1964 makes it unlawful for employers subject to the Act to discriminate on the basis of a person's "race, color, religion, sex, or national origin. . . ." 42 U.S.C. § 2000e–2(a). For many years, the courts of appeals of this country understood the prohibition against sex discrimination to exclude discrimination on the basis of a person's sexual orientation. The Supreme Court, however, has never spoken to that question. In this case, we have been asked to take a fresh look at our position in light of developments at the Supreme Court extending over two decades. We have done so, and we conclude today that discrimination on the basis of sexual orientation is a form of sex discrimination. We therefore reverse the district court's judgment dismissing Kimberly Hively's suit against Ivy Tech Community College and remand for further proceedings.

I

Hively is openly lesbian. She began teaching as a part-time, adjunct professor at Ivy Tech Community College's South Bend campus in 2000. Hoping to improve her lot, she applied for at least six full-time positions between 2009 and 2014. These efforts were unsuccessful; worse yet, in July 2014 her part-time contract was not renewed. Believing that Ivy Tech was spurning her because of her sexual orientation . . . .

After receiving a right-to-sue letter, she filed this action in the district court (again acting pro se). Ivy Tech responded with a motion to dismiss for failure to state a claim on which relief can be granted. It argued that sexual orientation is not a protected class under Title VII . . . . Relying on a line of this court's cases exemplified by *Hamner v. St. Vincent Hosp. and Health Care Ctr., Inc.*, 224 F.3d 701 (7th Cir. 2000), the district court granted Ivy Tech's motion and dismissed Hively's case with prejudice.

Now represented by the Lambda Legal Defense & Education Fund, Hively has appealed to this court. After an exhaustive exploration of the law governing claims involving discrimination based on sexual orientation, the panel affirmed. *Hively v. Ivy Tech Cmty. Coll.*, 830 F.3d 698 (7th Cir. 2016). It began its analysis by noting that the idea that discrimination based on sexual orientation is somehow distinct from sex discrimination originated with dicta in *Ulane v. Eastern Airlines, Inc.*, 742 F.2d 1081 (7th Cir. 1984). *Ulane* stated (as if this resolved matters) that Title VII's prohibition against sex discrimination "implies that it is unlawful to discriminate against women because they are women and against men because they are men." *Id.* at 1085. From this truism, we deduced that "Congress had nothing more than the traditional notion of 'sex' in mind when it voted to outlaw sex discrimination. . . ." *Doe v. City of Belleville, Ill.*, 119 F.3d 563, 572 (7th Cir. 1997), *cert. granted, judgment vacated sub nom. City of Belleville v. Doe*, 523 U.S. 1001, *abrogated by Oncale v. Sundowner Offshore Servs., Inc.*, 523 U.S. 75 (1998).

Later cases in this court, including *Hamm v. Weyauwega Milk Prods.*, 332 F.3d 1058 (7th Cir. 2003), *Hamner*, and *Spearman v. Ford Motor Co.*, 231 F.3d 1080, 1085 (7th Cir. 2000), have accepted this as settled law. Almost all of our sister circuits have understood the law in the same way. See, *e.g., Higgins v. New Balance Athletic Shoe, Inc.*, 194 F.3d 252, 259 (1st Cir. 1999); *Dawson v. Bumble & Bumble*, 398 F.3d 211, 217 (2d Cir. 2005); *Prowel v. Wise Bus. Forms, Inc.*, 579 F.3d 285, 290 (3d Cir. 2009); *Wrightson v. Pizza Hut of Am., Inc.*, 99 F.3d 138, 143 (4th Cir. 1996); *Blum v. Gulf Oil Corp.*, 597 F.2d 936, 938 (5th Cir. 1979); *Kalich v. AT&T Mobility, LLC*, 679 F.3d 464, 471 (6th Cir. 2012); *Williamson v. A.G. Edwards & Sons, Inc.*, 876 F.2d 69, 70 (8th Cir. 1989); *Medina v. Income Support Div.*, 413 F.3d 1131, 1135 (10th Cir. 2005); *Fredette v. BVP Mgmt. Assocs.*, 112 F.3d 1503, 1510 (11th Cir. 1997). A panel of the Eleventh Circuit, recognizing that it was bound by the Fifth Circuit's precedent in *Blum*, 597 F.2d 936, recently reaffirmed (by a 2–1 vote) that it could not recognize sexual orientation discrimination claims under Title VII. *Evans v. Georgia Reg'l Hosp.*, 850 F.3d 1248, 1255–57 (11th Cir. 2017). On the other hand, the Second Circuit recently found that an openly gay male plaintiff pleaded a claim of gender stereotyping that was sufficient to survive dismissal. The court observed that one panel lacked the power to reconsider the court's earlier decision holding that sexual orientation discrimination claims were not cognizable under Title VII. *Christiansen v. Omnicom Group, Inc.*, 852 F.3d 195 (2d Cir. 2017) (per curiam). Nonetheless, two of the three judges, relying on many of the same arguments presented here, noted in concurrence that they thought their court ought to consider revisiting that precedent in an appropriate case. *Id.* at 198–99 (Katzmann, J., concurring). Notable in its absence from the debate over the proper interpretation of the scope of Title VII's ban on sex discrimination is the United States Supreme Court.

That is not because the Supreme Court has left this subject entirely to the side. To the contrary, as the panel recognized, over the years the Court has issued several opinions that are relevant to the issue before us. Key among those decisions are *Price Waterhouse v. Hopkins*, 490 U.S. 228 and *Oncale v. Sundowner Offshore Servs., Inc.*, 523 U.S. 75 (1998). *Price Waterhouse* held that the practice of gender stereotyping falls within Title VII's prohibition against sex discrimination, and *Oncale* clarified that it makes no difference if the sex of the harasser is (or is not) the same as the sex of the victim. Our panel frankly acknowledged how difficult it is "to extricate the gender nonconformity claims from the sexual orientation claims." 830 F.3d at 709. That effort, it commented, has led to a "confused hodge-podge of cases." *Id.* at 711. It also noted that "all gay, lesbian and bisexual persons fail to comply with the sine qua non of gender stereotypes—that all men should form intimate relationships only with women, and all women should form intimate relationships only with men." *Id.* Especially since the Supreme Court's recognition that the Due Process and Equal Protection Clauses of the Constitution protect the right of same-sex couples to marry, *Obergefell v. Hodges,* ___ U.S. ___, 135 S.Ct. 2584 (2015), bizarre results ensue from the current regime. As the panel noted, it creates "a paradoxical legal landscape in which a person can be married on Saturday and then fired on Monday for just that act." 830 F.3d at 714. Finally, the panel highlighted the sharp tension between a rule that fails to recognize that discrimination on the basis of the sex with whom a person associates is a form of sex discrimination, and the rule, recognized since *Loving v. Virginia,* 388 U.S. 1 (1967), that discrimination on the basis of the race with whom a person associates is a form of racial discrimination.

Despite all these problems, the panel correctly noted that it was bound by this court's precedents, to which we referred earlier. It thought that the handwriting signaling their demise might be on the wall, but it did not feel empowered to translate that message into a holding. "Until the writing comes in the form of a Supreme Court opinion or new legislation," 830 F.3d at 718, it felt bound to adhere to our earlier decisions. In light of the importance of the issue, and recognizing the power of t42he full court to overrule earlier decisions and to bring our law into conformity with the Supreme Court's teachings, a majority of the judges in regular active service voted to rehear this case en banc.

II

A

The question before us is not whether this court can, or should, "amend" Title VII to add a new protected category to the familiar list of "race, color, religion, sex, or national origin." 42 U.S.C. § 2000e–2(a). Obviously that lies beyond our power. We must decide instead what it means to discriminate on the basis of sex, and in particular, whether actions taken on the basis of sexual orientation are a subset of actions taken on the basis of sex. This is a pure question of statutory interpretation and thus well within the judiciary's competence.

* * *

Ivy Tech sets great store on the fact that Congress has frequently considered amending Title VII to add the words "sexual orientation" to the list of prohibited characteristics, yet it has never done so. Many of our sister circuits have also noted this fact. In our view, however, it is simply too difficult to draw a reliable inference from these truncated legislative initiatives to rest our opinion on them. The goalposts have been moving over the years, as the Supreme Court has shed more light on the scope of the language that already is in the statute: no *sex* discrimination.

The dissent makes much of the fact that Congresses acting more than thirty years after the passage of Title VII made use of the term "sexual orientation" to prohibit discrimination or violence on that basis in statutes such as the Violence Against Women Act and the federal Hate Crimes Act. But this gets us no closer to answering the question at hand, for Congress may certainly choose to use both a belt and suspenders to achieve its objectives, and the fact that "sex" and "sexual orientation" discrimination may overlap in later statutes is of no help in determining whether sexual orientation discrimination *is* discrimination on the basis of sex for the purposes of Title VII. See, *e.g.*, *McEvoy v. IEI Barge Servs., Inc.*, 622 F.3d 671, 677 (7th Cir. 2010) ("Congress may choose a belt-and-suspenders approach to promote its policy objectives. . . .").

Moreover, the agency most closely associated with this law, the Equal Employment Opportunity Commission, in 2015 announced that it now takes the position that Title VII's prohibition against sex discrimination encompasses discrimination on the basis of sexual orientation. See *Baldwin v. Foxx*, EEOC Appeal No. 0120133080, 2015 WL 4397641 (July 15, 2015). Our point here is not that we have a duty to defer to the EEOC's position. We assume for present purposes that no such duty exists. But the Commission's position may have caused some in Congress to think that legislation is needed to carve sexual orientation *out* of the statute, not to put it *in*. In the end, we have no idea what inference to draw from congressional inaction or later enactments, because there is no way of knowing what explains each individual member's votes, much less what explains the failure of the body as a whole to change this 1964 statute.

* * *

It is therefore neither here nor there that the Congress that enacted the Civil Rights Act in 1964 and chose to include sex as a prohibited basis for employment discrimination (no matter why it did so) may not have realized or understood the full scope of the words it chose. Indeed, in the years since 1964, Title VII has been understood to cover far more than the simple decision of an employer not to hire a woman for Job A, or a man for Job B. The Supreme Court has held that the prohibition against sex discrimination reaches sexual harassment in the workplace, see *Meritor Sav. Bank, FSB v. Vinson*, 477 U.S. 57 (1986), including same-sex workplace harassment, see *Oncale*; it reaches discrimination based on actuarial assumptions about a person's longevity, see *City of Los Angeles, Dep't of Water and Power v. Manhart*, 435 U.S. 702 (1978); and it reaches discrimination based on a person's failure to conform to a certain set of gender stereotypes, see *Hopkins*. It is quite possible that these interpretations may also have surprised some who served in the 88th Congress. Nevertheless, experience with the law has led the

Supreme Court to recognize that each of these examples is a covered form of sex discrimination.

B

Hively offers two approaches in support of her contention that "sex discrimination" includes discrimination on the basis of sexual orientation. The first relies on the tried-and-true comparative method in which we attempt to isolate the significance of the plaintiff's sex to the employer's decision: has she described a situation in which, holding all other things constant and changing only her sex, she would have been treated the same way? The second relies on the *Loving v. Virginia*, 388 U.S. 1, 87 S.Ct. 1817, 18 L.Ed.2d 1010 (1967), line of cases, which she argues protect her right to associate intimately with a person of the same sex. Although the analysis differs somewhat, both avenues end up in the same place: sex discrimination.

1

* * *

Hively alleges that if she had been a man married to a woman (or living with a woman, or dating a woman) and everything else had stayed the same, Ivy Tech would not have refused to promote her and would not have fired her. . . . This describes paradigmatic sex discrimination. To use the phrase from *Ulane*, Ivy Tech is disadvantaging her *because she is a woman*. Nothing in the complaint hints that Ivy Tech has an anti-marriage policy that extends to heterosexual relationships, or for that matter even an anti-partnership policy that is gender-neutral.

Viewed through the lens of the gender non-conformity line of cases, Hively represents the ultimate case of failure to conform to the female stereotype (at least as understood in a place such as modern America, which views heterosexuality as the norm and other forms of sexuality as exceptional): she is not heterosexual. Our panel described the line between a gender nonconformity claim and one based on sexual orientation as gossamer-thin; we conclude that it does not exist at all. Hively's claim is no different from the claims brought by women who were rejected for jobs in traditionally male workplaces, such as fire departments, construction, and policing. The employers in those cases were policing the boundaries of what jobs or behaviors they found acceptable for a woman (or in some cases, for a man).

* * *

The virtue of looking at comparators and paying heed to gender non-conformity is that this process sheds light on the interpretive question raised by Hively's case: is sexual-orientation discrimination a form of sex discrimination, given the way in which the Supreme Court has interpreted the word "sex" in the statute? The dissent criticizes us for not trying to *rule out* sexual-orientation discrimination by controlling for it in our comparator example and for not placing any weight on the fact that if someone had asked Ivy Tech what its reasons were at the time of the discriminatory conduct, it probably would have said "sexual orientation," not "sex." We assume that this is true, but this thought experiment does not answer the question before us—instead, it begs that question. It commits the logical fallacy of assuming the conclusion it sets out to prove. It makes no sense to control for or rule out discrimination on the basis of sexual orientation if the question before us is *whether* that type of discrimination is nothing more or less than a form of sex discrimination. Repeating that the two are different, as the dissent does at numerous points, also does not advance the analysis.

2

As we noted earlier, Hively also has argued that action based on sexual orientation is sex discrimination under the associational theory. It is now accepted that a person who is discriminated against because of the protected characteristic of one with whom she associates is actually being disadvantaged because of her own traits. This line of cases began with *Loving*, in which the Supreme Court held that "restricting the freedom to marry solely because of racial classifications violates the central meaning of the Equal Protection Clause." 388 U.S. at 12. The Court rejected the argument that miscegenation statutes do not violate equal protection because they "punish equally both the white and the Negro participants in an interracial marriage." *Id.* at 8. When dealing with a statute containing racial classifications, it wrote, "the fact of equal application does not immunize the statute from the very heavy burden of justification" required by the Fourteenth Amendment for lines drawn by race. *Id.* at 9.

* * *

The dissent would instead have us compare the treatment of men who are attracted to members of the male sex with the treatment of women who are attracted to members of the female sex, and ask whether an employer treats the men differently from the women. But even setting to one side the logical fallacy involved, *Loving* shows why this fails. In the context of interracial relationships, we could just as easily hold constant a variable such as "sexual or romantic attraction to persons of a different race" and ask whether an employer treated persons of different races who shared that propensity the same. That is precisely the rule that *Loving* rejected, and so too must we, in the context of sexual associations.

The fact that *Loving* . . . dealt with racial associations, as opposed to those based on color, national origin, religion, or sex, is of no moment. The text of the statute draws no distinction, for this purpose, among the different varieties of discrimination it addresses—a fact recognized by the *Hopkins* plurality. See 490 U.S. at 244 n.9. This means that to the extent that the statute prohibits discrimination on the basis of the race of someone with whom the plaintiff associates, it also prohibits discrimination on the basis of the national origin, or the color, or the religion, or (as relevant here) the sex of the associate. No matter which category is involved, the essence of the claim is that the *plaintiff* would not be suffering the adverse action had his or her sex, race, color, national origin, or religion been different.

III

Today's decision must be understood against the backdrop of the Supreme Court's decisions, not only in the field of employment discrimination, but also in the area of broader discrimination on the basis of sexual orientation. We already have discussed the employment cases, especially *Hopkins* and *Oncale*. The latter line of cases began with *Romer v. Evans*, 517 U.S. 620 (1996), in which the Court held that a provision of the Colorado Constitution forbidding any organ of government in the state from taking action designed to protect "homosexual, lesbian, or bisexual" persons, *id.* at 624, violated the federal Equal Protection Clause. *Romer* was followed by *Lawrence v. Texas*, 539 U.S. 558 (2003), in which the Court found that a Texas statute criminalizing homosexual intimacy between consenting adults violated the liberty provision of the Due Process Clause. Next came *United States v. Windsor*, ___ U.S. ___, 133 S.Ct. 2675 (2013), which addressed the constitutionality of the part of the Defense of Marriage Act (DOMA) that excluded a same-sex partner from the definition of "spouse" in other federal statutes. The Court held that this part of DOMA "violate[d] basic due process and equal protection principles applicable to the Federal Government." *Id.* at 2693. Finally, the Court's decision in *Obergefell*, *supra*, held that the right to marry is a fundamental liberty right, protected by the Due Process and Equal Protection Clauses of the Fourteenth Amendment. 135 S.Ct. at 2604. The Court wrote that "[i]t is now clear that the challenged laws burden the liberty of same-sex couples, and it must be further acknowledged that they abridge central precepts of equality." *Id.*

It would require considerable calisthenics to remove the "sex" from "sexual orientation." The effort to do so has led to confusing and contradictory results, as our panel opinion illustrated so well. The EEOC concluded, in its *Baldwin* decision, that such an effort cannot be reconciled with the straightforward language of Title VII. Many district courts have come to the same conclusion. See, *e.g.*, *Boutillier v. Hartford Pub. Sch.*, No. 3:13-CV-01303-WWE, ___ F.Supp.3d ___, 2016 WL 6818348 (D. Conn. Nov. 17, 2016); *U.S. Equal Emp't Opportunity Comm'n v. Scott Med. Ctr., P.C.*, No. CV 16-225, ___ F.Supp.3d ___, 2016 WL 6569233 (W.D. Pa. Nov. 4, 2016); *Winstead v. Lafayette Cnty. Bd. of Cnty. Comm'rs*, 197 F.Supp.3d 1334 (N.D. Fla. 2016); *Isaacs v. Felder Servs., LLC*, 143 F.Supp.3d 1190 (M.D. Ala. 2015); see also *Videckis v. Pepperdine Univ.*, 150 F.Supp.3d 1151 (C.D. Cal. 2015) (Title IX case, applying Title VII principles and *Baldwin*). Many other courts have found that gender-identity claims are cognizable under Title VII. See, *e.g.*, *Rosa v. Park W. Bank & Tr. Co.*, 214 F.3d 213, 215–16 (1st Cir. 2000) (claim for sex discrimination under Equal Credit Opportunity Act, analogizing to Title VII); *Schwenk v. Hartford*, 204 F.3d 1187, 1201–02 (9th Cir. 2000) (relying on Title VII cases to conclude that violence against a transsexual was violence because of gender under the Gender Motivated Violence Act); *Barnes v. City of Cincinnati*, 401 F.3d 729 (6th Cir. 2005); *Smith v. City of Salem, Ohio*, 378 F.3d 566 (6th Cir. 2004); *Fabian v. Hosp. of Cent. Conn.*, 172 F.Supp.3d 509 (D. Conn. 2016); *Schroer v. Billington*, 577 F.Supp.2d 293, 308 (D.D.C. 2008).

* * *

. . . We hold only that a person who alleges that she experienced employment discrimination on the basis of her sexual orientation has put forth a case of sex discrimination for Title VII purposes. It was therefore wrong to dismiss Hively's complaint for failure to state a claim. The judgment of the district court is REVERSED and the case is REMANDED for further proceedings.

NOTES AND QUESTIONS

1.   Traditionally, federal courts have distinguished discrimination based on sex from discrimination based on sexual orientation and held that the latter did not constitute discrimination based on sex. Under the Obama Administration, the EEOC pushed the argument that discrimination based on sexual orientation is a form of discrimination based on sex. See EEOC Press Release, EEOC Files First Suits Challenging Sexual Orientation Discrimination as Sex Discrimination (3/1/16), available at https://www.eeoc.gov/eeoc/newsroom/release/3-1-16.cfm. In Baldwin v. Foxx, EEOC Doc. 0120133080, 2015 WL 4397641 (July 15, 2015), the EEOC collapsed the distinction between sex and sexual orientation discrimination holding that discrimination based on sexual orientation is a form of sex discrimination. In *Hively*, the en banc Seventh Circuit reversed its own precedent to become the first circuit court to agree with the EEOC and hold that discrimination based on sexual orientation is actionable sex discrimination. Other courts have maintained the distinction between sex and sexual orientation holding that only the former is actionable under Title VII. See Evans v. Georgia Reg'l Hosp., 850 F.3d 1248 (11th Cir. 2017) (holding that discrimination based on sexual orientation is not actionable under Title VII, though discrimination based on failure to conform to a gender stereotype is); Hinton v. Virginia Union Univ., 2016 WL 2621967 at 5 (E.D. Va., May 5, 2016) (holding that "Title VII does not encompass sexual orientation discrimination claims, and cannot be supplanted by the merely persuasive power of the EEOC's decision"); Simonton v. Runyon, 232 F.3d 33, 35 (2d Cir. 2000) (rejecting plaintiff's argument that discrimination based on sex includes discrimination based on sexual orientation); but see Franchina v. City of Providence, 881 F.3d 32 (1st Cir. 2018) (holding that Title VII does not "foreclose[ ] a plaintiff in our Circuit from bringing sex-plus claims under Title VII where in addition to the sex-based charge, the "plus" factor is the plaintiff's status as a gay or lesbian individual"). From the perspective of legal logic, does it make sense to treat discrimination based on sexual

orientation as a form of sex discrimination or as a distinct form of discrimination? From a policy standpoint, which approach is most appropriate?

2. Employees have also been unsuccessful establishing a Title VII violation for religious discrimination based on sexual orientation discrimination. See Prowel v. Wise Bus. Forms, Inc., 579 F.3d 285 (3d Cir. 2009) (held: no claim for religious discrimination under Title VII where homosexual employee claimed he was harassed for failing to conform to his employer's religious beliefs).

3. Although courts have held that discrimination based on sexual orientation does not violate Title VII, sexual orientation does not preclude an employee from establishing a valid Title VII claim for harassment based on sex where the alleged harasser is of the same sex. See Ellsworth v. Pot Luck Enters., Inc., 624 F. Supp. 2d 868 (M.D. Tenn. 2009).

4. About half of the states, the District of Columbia, and numerous cities have enacted laws prohibiting discrimination in private employment on the basis of sexual orientation. In Underwood v. Archer Mgmt. Servs. Inc., 857 F. Supp. 96 (D.D.C. 1994), the court held that the District of Columbia's law prohibiting discrimination based on sexual orientation did not extend to transsexuals, although a discharge based on the plaintiff's masculine appearance stated a claim for discrimination based on the D.C. statute prohibiting discrimination based on personal appearance.

5. In Romer v. Evans, 517 U.S. 620 (1996), the Supreme Court, 6–3, held that Colorado's "Amendment 2" was unconstitutional. The amendment invalidated all existing and *future* state and local legislative, executive, or judicial action in Colorado, including those dealing with employment, that protect homosexuals from discrimination. In holding that Amendment 2 violated Equal Protection, Justice Kennedy wrote that Amendment 2 "seems inexplicable by anything but animus toward the class it affects." State efforts to limit the expansion of antidiscrimination protection have not ended however, but only changed forms. In 2015, Arkansas passed the Intrastate Commerce Improvement Act prohibiting local governments from providing protections against discrimination that exceeded those provided by state law. Ark. Code § 14–1–403. The Act was passed in response to a City of Fayetville ordinance prohibiting discrimination in employment and housing based on sexual orientation and gender identity. Tennessee passed similar legislation, the Equal Access to Intrastate Commerce Act, in 2011. T.C.A. § 7–51–1801. In Howe v. Haslam, 2014 WL 5698877 (Tenn. Ct. App., Nov. 4, 2014), the Tennessee Court of Appeals upheld that state's law against an equal protection challenge and distinguished the law from that at issue in *Romer*. In 2016, North Carolina passed a law preempting any local workplace anti-discrimination ordinances. See H.R. 2, 2016 Gen. Assemb., 2d Extra Sess. (N.C. 2016).

6. In Goins v. West Group, 635 N.W.2d 717 (Minn. 2001), however, a former employee was unsuccessful in a claim of sexual orientation discrimination under state law. The Minnesota Supreme Court held that an employer did not violate the law's prohibition on sexual orientation discrimination by designating employee restroom use on the basis of biological gender rather than "self-image" gender.

PART III

TERMS AND CONDITIONS OF EMPLOYMENT

CHAPTER 5

WAGES AND HOURS

A. FEDERAL AND STATE WAGE AND HOUR REGULATION

1. FEDERAL WAGE AND HOUR REGULATION: THE FAIR LABOR STANDARDS ACT

b. BASIC PROVISIONS OF THE FAIR LABOR STANDARDS ACT

(i) Minimum Wage

Page 439. Substitute the following for the last full paragraph on the page.

As of June 2018, 29 states and the District of Columbia have minimum wages higher than that required by federal law, and thirteen of them have hourly minimums of $10 or more. Further, a list of cities have higher minimum wages than the states in which they are located; for example, the city of SeaTac, Washington was the first city in the country to adopt a $15/hour minimum wage, in late 2013. However, as discussed at greater length later in the chapter, states may preempt local wage laws.

(ii) Overtime

Page 441. Please insert as new notes.

3. California has a "day of rest" statute. That law prohibits an employer from "causing employees to work more than six days in seven" but does not apply "when the total hours of employment do not exceed 30 hours in any week or six hours in any one day thereof." If the employer fails to comply, it will have to pay the relevant workers an "overtime premium." For interpretation of the complicated ambiguities of this statute, some sections of which go back to 1858, see Mendoza v. Nordstrom, Inc., 393 P.3d 375 (Cal. 2017).

4. A handful of cities have enacted what are sometimes called "secure scheduling laws," which are aimed at promoting predictable and stable work schedules for low wage workers. For example, in 2015, San Francisco enacted a law requiring "formula retail" businesses to pay workers a premium for last-minute schedule changes or for requiring workers to be "on call."

c. COVERAGE

(i) Who Is a Covered Employer?

Page 444. Please add a new note.

6. What happens when there is more than one entity that is arguably responsible for complying with the FLSA? In Hall v. DIRECTV, 846 F.3d 757 (4th Cir. 2017), the court considered whether DIRECTV or one of its subsidiaries was a "joint employer" of the plaintiffs, who were technicians charged with installing satellite TV systems. According to the complaint in the case, DIRECTV contracted with "Home Service Providers," which in turn contracted with subcontractors, which then hired the technicians. However, the complaint further alleged that DIRECTV controlled nearly every aspect of the technicians' work, including the uniforms they wore, their training, and their work assignments. The Fourth Circuit held that the plaintiffs had stated a claim that DIRECTV was their joint employer under its test, which considers whether the putative joint employer "(1) had the power to hire and fire the employee; (2) supervised and controlled employee work schedules or conditions of employment; (3) determined the rate and method of payment; and (4) maintained employment records.

(ii) Who Is a Covered Employee?

(a) Who Is an Employee?

Page 453. Please insert before Note 7; Add a 'Notes and Questions' heading and make Notes 7 and 8 into Notes 1 and 2.

Glatt v. Fox Searchlight Pictures, Inc.

811 F.3d 528 (2d Cir. 2015).

■ JOHN M. WALKER, JR., CIRCUIT JUDGE:

Plaintiffs, who were hired as unpaid interns, claim compensation as employees under the Fair Labor Standards Act and New York Labor Law. Plaintiffs Eric Glatt and Alexander Footman moved for partial summary judgment on their employment status. Plaintiff Eden Antalik moved to certify a class of all New York interns working at certain of defendants' divisions between 2005 and 2010 and to conditionally certify a nationwide collective of all interns working at those same divisions between 2008 and 2010. The district court granted Glatt and Footman's motion for partial summary judgment, certified Antalik's New York class, and conditionally certified Antalik's nationwide collective. On defendants' interlocutory appeal, we VACATE the district court's order granting partial summary judgment to Glatt and Footman, VACATE its order certifying Antalik's New York class, VACATE its order conditionally certifying Antalik's nationwide collective, and REMAND for further proceedings.

Plaintiffs worked as unpaid interns either on the Fox Searchlight-distributed film *Black Swan* or at the Fox corporate offices in New York City. They contend that the defendants, Fox Searchlight and Fox Entertainment Group, violated the Fair Labor Standards Act (FLSA) by failing to pay them as employees during their internships as required by the FLSA's and NYLL's minimum wage and overtime provisions. The following background facts are undisputed except where noted.

Eric Glatt graduated with a degree in multimedia instructional design from New York University. Glatt was enrolled in a non-matriculated (non-degree) graduate program at NYU's School of Education when he started working on *Black Swan*. His graduate program did not offer him credit for his internship.

From December 2, 2009, through the end of February 2010, Glatt interned in *Black Swan's* accounting department under the supervision of Production Accountant Theodore Au. He worked from approximately 9:00 a.m. to 7:00 p.m. five days a week. As an accounting intern, Glatt's responsibilities included copying, scanning, and filing documents; tracking purchase orders; transporting paperwork and items to and from the *Black Swan* set; maintaining employee personnel files; and answering questions about the accounting department.

Glatt interned a second time in *Black Swan's* post-production department from March 2010 to August 2010, under the supervision of Post Production Supervisor Jeff Robinson. Glatt worked two days a week from approximately 11:00 a.m. until 6:00 or 7:00 p.m. His post-production responsibilities included drafting cover letters for mailings; organizing filing cabinets; filing paperwork; making photocopies; keeping the take-out menus up-to-date and organized; bringing documents to the payroll company; and running errands, one of which required him to purchase a non-allergenic pillow for Director Darren Aronofsky.

Alexander Footman graduated from Wesleyan University with a degree in film studies. He was not enrolled in a degree program at the time of his *Black Swan* internship. From September 29, 2009, through late February or early March 2010, Footman interned in the production department under the supervision of Production Office Coordinator Lindsay Feldman and Assistant Production Office Coordinator Jodi Arneson. Footman worked approximately ten-hour days. At first, Footman worked five days a week, but, beginning in November 2009, he worked only three days a week. After this schedule change, *Black Swan* replaced Footman with another unpaid intern in the production department.

Footman's responsibilities included picking up and setting up office furniture; arranging lodging for cast and crew; taking out the trash; taking lunch orders; answering phone calls; watermarking scripts; drafting daily call sheets; photocopying; making coffee; making deliveries to and from the film production set, rental houses, and the payroll office; accepting deliveries; admitting guests to the office; compiling lists of local vendors; breaking down, removing, and selling office furniture and supplies at the end of production; internet research; sending invitations to the wrap party; and other similar tasks and errands, including bringing tea to Aronofsky and dropping off a DVD of *Black Swan* footage at Aronofsky's apartment.

Eden Antalik worked as an unpaid publicity intern in Fox Searchlight's corporate office in New York from the beginning of May 2009 until the second week of August 2009. During her internship, Antalik was enrolled in a degree program at Duquesne University that required her to have an internship in order to graduate.

Antalik was supposed to receive credit for her internship at Fox Searchlight, but, for reasons that are unclear from the record, she never actually received the credit. Antalik began work each morning around 8:00 a.m. by assembling a brief, referred to as "the breaks," summarizing mentions of various Fox Searchlight films in the media. She also made travel arrangements, organized catering, shipped documents, and set up rooms for press events.

* * *

On June 11, 2013, the district court concluded that Glatt and Footman had been improperly classified as unpaid interns rather than employees and granted their partial motion for summary judgment. The district court also granted Antalik's motions to certify the class of New York interns and to conditionally certify the nationwide FLSA collective.

* * *

At its core, this interlocutory appeal raises the broad question of under what circumstances an unpaid intern must be deemed an "employee" under the FLSA and therefore compensated for his work. That broad question underlies our answers to the three specific questions on appeal. First, did the district court apply the correct standard in evaluating whether Glatt and Footman were employees, and, if so, did it reach the correct result? Second, did the district court err by certifying Antalik's class of New York interns? Third, did the district court err by conditionally certifying Antalik's nationwide collective?

* * *

With certain exceptions not relevant here, the FLSA requires employers to pay all employees a specified minimum wage, and overtime of time and one-half for hours worked in excess of forty hours per week. NYLL requires the same, except that it specifies a higher wage rate than the federal minimum. An employee cannot waive his right to the minimum wage and overtime pay because waiver "would nullify the purposes of the [FLSA] and thwart the legislative policies it was designed to effectuate."

The strictures of both the FLSA and NYLL apply only to employees. The FLSA unhelpfully defines "employee" as an "individual employed by an employer." "Employ" is defined as "to suffer or permit to work." New York likewise defines "employee" as "any individual employed, suffered or permitted to work by an employer." Because the statutes define "employee" in nearly identical terms, we construe the NYLL definition as the same in substance as the definition in the FLSA.

The Supreme Court has yet to address the difference between unpaid interns and paid employees under the FLSA. In 1947, however, the Court recognized that unpaid railroad brakemen trainees should not be treated as employees, and thus that they were beyond the reach of the FLSA's minimum wage provision. The Court adduced several facts. First, the brakemen- trainees at issue did not displace any regular employees, and their work did not expedite the employer's business. Second, the brakemen-trainees did not expect to receive any compensation and would not necessarily be hired upon successful completion of the course. Third, the training course was similar to one offered by a vocational school. Finally, the employer received no immediate advantage from the work done by the trainees.

In 1967, the Department of Labor ("DOL") issued informal guidance on trainees as part of its Field Operations Handbook. The guidance enumerated six criteria and stated that the trainee is not an employee only if all of the criteria were met. In 2010, the DOL published similar guidance for unpaid interns working in the for-profit private sector. This Intern Fact Sheet provides that an employment relationship does not exist if all of the following factors apply:

1.   The internship, even though it includes actual operation of the facilities of the employer, is similar to training which would be given in an educational environment;

2.   The internship experience is for the benefit of the intern;

3.   The intern does not displace regular employees, but works under close supervision of existing staff;

4.   The employer that provides the training derives no immediate advantage from the activities of the intern; and on occasion its operations may actually be impeded;

5.   The intern is not necessarily entitled to a job at the conclusion of the internship; and

6.   The employer and the intern understand that the intern is not entitled to wages for the time spent in the internship.

The district court evaluated Glatt's and Footman's employment using a version of the DOL's six-factor test. However, the district court, unlike the DOL, did not explicitly require that all six factors be present to establish that the intern is not an employee and instead balanced the factors. The district court found that the first four factors weighed in favor of finding that Glatt and Footman were employees and the last two factors favored finding them to be trainees. As a result, the district court concluded that Glatt and Footman had been improperly classified as unpaid interns and granted their motion for partial summary judgment.

The specific issue we face—when is an unpaid intern entitled to compensation as an employee under the FLSA?—is a matter of first impression in this Circuit. When properly designed, unpaid internship programs can greatly benefit interns. For this reason, internships are widely supported by educators and by employers looking to hire well-trained recent graduates. However, employers can also exploit unpaid interns by using their free labor without providing them with an appreciable benefit in education or experience. Recognizing this concern, all parties agree that there are circumstances in which someone who is labeled an unpaid intern is actually an employee entitled to compensation under the FLSA. All parties also agree that there are circumstances in which unpaid interns are not employees under the FLSA. They do not agree on what those circumstances are or what standard we should use to identify them.

The plaintiffs urge us to adopt a test whereby interns will be considered employees whenever the employer receives an immediate advantage from the interns' work. Plaintiffs argue that focusing on any immediate advantage that accrues to the employer is appropriate because, in their view, the Supreme Court in [1947] rested its holding on the finding that the brakemen trainees provided no immediate advantage to the employer.

The defendants urge us to adopt a more nuanced primary beneficiary test. Under this standard, an employment relationship is created when the tangible and intangible benefits provided to the intern are greater than the intern's contribution to the employer's operation. They argue that the primary beneficiary test best reflects the economic realities of the relationship between intern and employer. They further contend that a primary beneficiary test that considers the totality of the circumstances is in accordance with how we decide whether individuals are employees in other circumstances.

DOL, appearing as amicus curiae in support of the plaintiffs, defends the six factors enumerated in its Intern Fact Sheet and its requirement that every factor be present before the employer can escape its obligation to pay the worker. DOL argues (1) that its views on employee status are entitled to deference because it is the agency charged with administering the FLSA and (2) that we should use the six factors because they come directly from [the Supreme Court].

We decline DOL's invitation to defer to the test laid out in the Intern Fact Sheet.

* * *

Instead, we agree with defendants that the proper question is whether the intern or the employer is the primary beneficiary of the relationship. The primary beneficiary test has two salient features. First, it focuses on what the intern receives in exchange for his work. Second, it also accords courts the flexibility to examine the economic reality as it exists between the intern and the employer.

Although the flexibility of the primary beneficiary test is primarily a virtue, this virtue is not unalloyed. The defendants' conception of the primary beneficiary test requires courts to weigh a diverse set of benefits to the intern against an equally diverse set of benefits received by the employer without specifying the relevance of particular facts.

In somewhat analogous contexts, we have articulated a set of non-exhaustive factors to aid courts in determining whether a worker is an employee for purposes of the FLSA. In the context of unpaid internships, we think a non-exhaustive set of considerations should include:

1. The extent to which the intern and the employer clearly understand that there is no expectation of compensation. Any promise of compensation, express or implied, suggests that the intern is an employee—and vice versa.

2. The extent to which the internship provides training that would be similar to that which would be given in an educational environment, including the clinical and other hands-on training provided by educational institutions.

3. The extent to which the internship is tied to the intern's formal education program by integrated coursework or the receipt of academic credit.

4. The extent to which the internship accommodates the intern's academic commitments by corresponding to the academic calendar.

5. The extent to which the internship's duration is limited to the period in which the internship provides the intern with beneficial learning.

6. The extent to which the intern's work complements, rather than displaces, the work of paid employees while providing significant educational benefits to the intern.

7. The extent to which the intern and the employer understand that the internship is conducted without entitlement to a paid job at the conclusion of the internship.

Applying these considerations requires weighing and balancing all of the circumstances. No one factor is dispositive and every factor need not point in the same direction for the court to conclude that the intern is not an employee entitled to the minimum wage. In addition, the factors we specify are non-exhaustive—courts may consider relevant evidence beyond the specified factors in appropriate cases.

* * *

The approach we adopt also reflects a central feature of the modern internship—the relationship between the internship and the intern's formal education. The purpose of a bona-fide internship is to integrate classroom learning with practical skill development in a real-world setting, and, * * * all of the plaintiffs were enrolled in or had recently completed a formal course of post-secondary education. By focusing on the educational aspects of the internship, our approach better reflects the role of internships in today's economy than the DOL factors, which were derived from a 68-year old Supreme Court decision that dealt with a single training course offered to prospective railroad brakemen.

In sum, we agree with the defendants that the proper question is whether the intern or the employer is the primary beneficiary of the relationship, and we propose the above list of non-exhaustive factors to aid courts in answering that question. The district court limited its review to the six factors in DOL's Intern Fact Sheet. Therefore, we vacate the district court's order granting partial summary judgment to Glatt and Footman and remand for further proceedings. On remand, the district court may, in its discretion, permit the parties to submit additional evidence relevant to the plaintiffs' employment status, such as evidence on Glatt's and Footman's formal education. Of course, we express no opinion with respect to the outcome of any renewed motions for summary judgment the parties might make based on the primary beneficiary test we have set forth.

* * *

For the foregoing reasons, the district court's orders are VACATED and the case REMANDED for further proceedings consistent with this opinion.

* * *

Page 455. Please insert the following before what is now Note 8 and make Note 8 into Note 9.

8.   In Acosta v. Cathedral Buffet, 887 F.3d 761 (6th Cir. 2018), the court held that unpaid church members who worked at a church-operated restaurant were not employees because they did not expect to be paid. The possibility that church members worked in the restaurant due to "spiritual coercion"—they were reportedly told that refusing to volunteer was an "unforgivable sin"—was not enough to qualify as an expectation of remuneration.

(b)   Exempt Employees

Page 460. Please add the following new case before the Note 1.

The following case made two trips to the Supreme Court. This is the most recent opinion, issued April 2, 2018.

Encino Motorcars v. Navarro

138 S.Ct. 1134 (2018).

■ JUSTICE THOMAS delivered the opinion of the Court.

The Fair Labor Standards Act (FLSA), 52 Stat. 1060, as amended, 29 U.S.C. § 201 et seq., requires employers to pay overtime compensation to covered employees. The FLSA exempts from the overtime-pay requirement "any salesman, partsman, or mechanic primarily engaged in selling or servicing automobiles" at a covered dealership. § 213(b)(10)(A). We granted certiorari to decide whether this exemption applies to service advisors—employees at car dealerships who consult with customers about their servicing needs and sell them servicing solutions. We conclude that service advisors are exempt.

I.

A.

Enacted in 1938, the FLSA requires employers to pay overtime to covered employees who work more than 40 hours in a week. 29 U.S.C. § 207(a). But the FLSA exempts many categories of employees from this requirement. See § 213. Employees at car dealerships have long been among those exempted.

Congress initially exempted all employees at car dealerships from the overtime-pay requirement. See Fair Labor Standards Amendments of 1961, § 9. Congress then narrowed that exemption to cover "any salesman, partsman, or mechanic primarily engaged in selling or servicing automobiles, trailers, trucks, farm implements, or aircraft." Fair Labor Standards Amendments of 1966, § 209. In 1974, Congress enacted the version of the exemption at issue here. It provides that the FLSA's overtime-pay requirement does not apply to "any salesman, partsman, or mechanic primarily engaged in selling or servicing automobiles, trucks, or farm implements, if he is employed by a nonmanufacturing establishment primarily engaged in the business of selling such vehicles or implements to ultimate purchasers." § 213(b)(10)(A).

This language has long been understood to cover service advisors. Although the Department of Labor initially interpreted it to exclude them, the federal courts rejected that view. After these decisions, the Department issued an opinion letter in 1978, explaining that service advisors are exempt in most cases. From 1978 to 2011, Congress made no changes to the exemption, despite amending § 213 nearly a dozen times. . . .

In 2011, however, the Department reversed course. It issued a rule that interpreted "salesman" to exclude service advisors. 76 Fed. Reg. 18832, 18859 (2011) (codified at 29 C.F.R. § 779.372(c)). That regulation prompted this litigation.

B.

Petitioner Encino Motorcars, LLC, is a Mercedes-Benz dealership in California. Respondents are current and former service advisors for petitioner. Service advisors "interact with customers and sell them services for their vehicles." Encino Motorcars, LLC v. Navarro, 136 S.Ct. 2117, 2121 (2016) (*Encino I*). They "mee[t] customers; liste[n] to their concerns about their cars; sugges[t] repair and maintenance services; sel[l] new accessories or replacement parts; recor[d] service orders; follo[w] up with customers as the services are performed (for instance, if new problems are discovered); and explai[n] the repair and maintenance work when customers return for their vehicles."

In 2012, respondents sued petitioner for backpay. Relying on the Department's 2011 regulation, respondents alleged that petitioner had violated the FLSA by failing to pay them overtime. Petitioner moved to dismiss, arguing that service advisors are exempt under § 213(b)(10)(A). The District Court agreed with petitioner and dismissed the complaint, but the Court of Appeals for the Ninth Circuit reversed. Finding the text ambiguous and the legislative history "inconclusive," the Ninth Circuit deferred to the Department's 2011 rule under Chevron U.S.A. Inc. v. Natural Resources Defense Council, Inc., 467 U.S. 837 (1984).

We granted certiorari and vacated the Ninth Circuit's judgment. We explained that courts cannot defer to the 2011 rule because it is procedurally defective. Specifically, the regulation undermined significant reliance interests in the automobile industry by changing the treatment of service advisors without a sufficiently reasoned explanation. But we did not decide whether, without administrative deference, the exemption covers service advisors. We remanded that issue for the Ninth Circuit to address in the first instance.

C.

On remand, the Ninth Circuit again held that the exemption does not include service advisors. The Court of Appeals agreed that a service advisor is a " 'salesman' " in a "generic sense," and is " 'primarily engaged in ... servicing automobiles' " in a "general sense." Nonetheless, it concluded that "Congress did not intend to exempt service advisors."

The Ninth Circuit began by noting that the Department's 1966–1967 Occupational Outlook Handbook listed 12 job titles in the table of contents that could be found at a car dealership, including "automobile mechanics," "automobile parts countermen," "automobile salesmen," and "automobile service advisors." Because the FLSA exemption listed three of these positions, but not service advisors, the Ninth Circuit concluded that service advisors are not exempt. The Ninth Circuit also determined that service advisors are not primarily engaged in "servicing" automobiles, which it defined to mean "only those who are actually occupied in the repair and maintenance of cars." And the Ninth Circuit further concluded that the exemption does not cover salesmen who are primarily engaged in servicing. In reaching this conclusion, the Ninth Circuit invoked the distributive canon. See A. Scalia & B. Garner, Reading Law 214 (2012) ("Distributive phrasing applies each expression to its appropriate referent"). It reasoned that "Congress intended the gerunds—selling and servicing—to be distributed to their appropriate subjects—salesman, partsman, and mechanic. A salesman sells; a partsman services; and a mechanic services." Finally, the Court of Appeals noted that its interpretation was supported by the principle that exemptions to the FLSA should be construed narrowly, and the lack of any "mention of service advisors" in the legislative history.

We granted certiorari, and now reverse.

II.

The FLSA exempts from its overtime-pay requirement "any salesman, partsman, or mechanic primarily engaged in selling or servicing automobiles, trucks, or farm implements, if he is employed by a nonmanufacturing establishment primarily engaged in the business of selling such vehicles or implements to ultimate purchasers." § 213(b)(10)(A). The parties agree that petitioner is a "nonmanufacturing establishment primarily engaged in the business of selling [automobiles] to ultimate purchasers." The parties also agree that a service advisor is not a "partsman" or "mechanic," and that a service advisor is not "primarily engaged . . . in selling automobiles." The question, then, is whether service advisors are "salesm[e]n . . . primarily engaged in . . . servicing automobiles." We conclude that they are. Under the best reading of the text, service advisors are "salesm[e]n," and they are "primarily engaged in . . . servicing automobiles." The distributive canon, the practice of construing FLSA exemptions narrowly, and the legislative history do not persuade us otherwise.

A.

A service advisor is obviously a "salesman." The term "salesman" is not defined in the statute, so "we give the term its ordinary meaning." The ordinary meaning of "salesman" is someone who sells goods or services. Service advisors do precisely that. As this Court previously explained, service advisors "sell [customers] services for their vehicles."

B.

Service advisors are also "primarily engaged in . . . servicing automobiles." § 213(b)(10)(A). The word "servicing" in this context can mean either "the action of maintaining or repairing a motor vehicle" or "[t]he action of providing a service." Service advisors satisfy both definitions. Service advisors are integral to the servicing process. They "mee[t] customers; liste[n] to their concerns about their cars; sugges[t] repair and maintenance services; sel[l] new accessories or replacement parts; recor[d] service orders; follo[w] up with customers as the services are performed (for instance, if new problems are discovered); and explai[n] the repair and maintenance work when customers return for their vehicles." If you ask the average customer who services his car, the primary, and perhaps only, person he is likely to identify is his service advisor.

True, service advisors do not spend most of their time physically repairing automobiles. But the statutory language is not so constrained. All agree that partsmen, for example, are "primarily engaged in . . . servicing automobiles." . . . In other words, the phrase "primarily engaged in . . . servicing automobiles" must include some individuals who do not physically repair automobiles themselves but who are integrally involved in the servicing process. That description applies to partsmen and service advisors alike.

C.

The Ninth Circuit concluded that service advisors are not covered because the exemption simply does not apply to "salesm[e]n . . . primarily engaged in . . . servicing automobiles." The Ninth Circuit invoked the distributive canon to reach this conclusion. Using that canon, it matched "salesman" with "selling" and "partsma[n] [and] mechanic" with "servicing." We reject this reasoning.

The text of the exemption covers "any salesman, partsman, or mechanic primarily engaged in selling or servicing automobiles, trucks, or farm implements." § 213(b)(10)(A). The exemption uses the word "or" to connect all of its nouns and gerunds, and "or" is "almost always disjunctive." Thus, the use of "or" to join "selling" and "servicing" suggests that the exemption covers a salesman primarily engaged in either activity.

Unsurprisingly, statutory context can overcome the ordinary, disjunctive meaning of "or." The distributive canon, for example, recognizes that sometimes "[w]here a sentence contains several antecedents and several consequents," courts should "read them distributively and apply the words to the subjects which, by context, they seem most properly to relate."

But here, context favors the ordinary disjunctive meaning of "or" for at least three reasons. First, the distributive canon has the most force when the statute allows for one-to-one matching. But here, the distributive canon would mix and match some of three nouns— "salesman, partsman, or mechanic"—with one of two gerunds—"selling or servicing." § 213(b)(10)(A). We doubt that a legislative drafter would leave it to the reader to figure out the precise combinations. Second, the distributive canon has the most force when an ordinary, disjunctive reading is linguistically impossible. But as explained above, the phrase "salesman . . . primarily engaged in . . . servicing automobiles" not only makes sense; it is an apt description of a service advisor. Third, a narrow distributive phrasing is an unnatural fit here because the entire exemption bespeaks breadth. It begins with the word "any." And it uses the disjunctive word "or" three times. In fact, all agree that the third list in the exemption—"automobiles, trucks, or farm implements"—modifies every other noun and gerund. But it would be odd to read the exemption as starting with a distributive phrasing and then, halfway through and without warning, switching to a disjunctive phrasing—all the while using the same word ("or") to signal both meanings. The more natural reading is that the exemption covers any combination of its nouns, gerunds, and objects.

D.

The Ninth Circuit also invoked the principle that exemptions to the FLSA should be construed narrowly. We reject this principle as a useful guidepost for interpreting the FLSA. Because the FLSA gives no "textual indication" that its exemptions should be construed narrowly, "there is no reason to give [them] anything other than a fair (rather than a 'narrow') interpretation." Scalia, Reading Law, at 363. The narrow-construction principle relies on the flawed premise that the FLSA " 'pursues' " its remedial purpose " 'at all costs.' " But the FLSA has over two dozen exemptions in § 213(b) alone, including the one at issue here. Those exemptions are as much a part of the FLSA's purpose as the overtime-pay requirement. We thus have no license to give the exemption anything but a fair reading.

* * *

In sum, we conclude that service advisors are exempt from the overtime-pay requirement of the FLSA because they are "salesm[e]n . . . primarily engaged in . . . servicing automobiles." § 213(b)(10)(A). Accordingly, we reverse the judgment of the Court of Appeals and remand the case for further proceedings consistent with this opinion.

It is so ordered.

■ JUSTICE GINSBURG, with whom JUSTICE BREYER, JUSTICE SOTOMAYOR, and JUSTICE KAGAN join, dissenting.

Diverse categories of employees staff automobile dealerships. Of employees so engaged, Congress explicitly exempted from the Fair Labor Standards Act hours requirements only three occupations: salesmen, partsmen, and mechanics. The Court today approves the exemption of a fourth occupation: automobile service advisors. In accord with the judgment of the Court of Appeals for the Ninth Circuit, I would not enlarge the exemption to include service advisors or other occupations outside Congress' enumeration.

* * *

"Where Congress explicitly enumerates certain exceptions . . ., additional exceptions are not to be implied, in the absence of evidence of a contrary legislative intent." The Court thus has no warrant to add to the three explicitly exempt categories (salesmen, partsmen, and mechanics) a fourth (service advisors) for which the Legislature did not provide. . . .

Had the § 213(b)(10)(A) exemption covered "any salesman or mechanic primarily engaged in selling or servicing automobiles," there could be no argument that service advisors fit within it. Only "salesmen" primarily engaged in "selling" automobiles and "mechanics" primarily engaged in "servicing" them would fall outside the Act's coverage. Service advisors, defined as "*salesmen* primarily engaged in the *selling of services*," plainly do not belong in either category. . . .

Petitioner stakes its case on Congress' addition of the "partsman" job to the exemption. That inclusion, petitioner urges, has a vacuum effect: It draws into the exemption job categories other than the three for which Congress provided, in particular, service advisors. Because partsmen, like service advisors, neither "sell" nor "service" automobiles in the conventional sense, petitioner reasons, Congress must have intended the word "service" to mean something broader than repair and maintenance.

To begin with, petitioner's premise is flawed. Unlike service advisors, partsmen " 'get their hands dirty' by 'working as a mechanic's right-hand man or woman.' " As the Solicitor General put it last time this case was before the Court, a mechanic "might be able to obtain the parts to complete a repair without the real-time assistance of a partsman by his side." But dividing the "key [repair] tasks . . . between two individuals" only "reinforces" "that both the mechanic and the partsman are . . . involved in repairing ('servicing') the vehicle." Service advisors, in contrast, "*sell . . . services* [to customers] for their vehicles," services that are later performed by mechanics and partsmen.

Adding partsmen to the exemption, moreover, would be an exceptionally odd way for Congress to have indicated that "servicing" should be given a meaning deviating from its ordinary usage. There is a more straightforward explanation for Congress' inclusion of partsmen alongside salesmen and mechanics: Common features of the three enumerated jobs make them unsuitable for overtime pay.

* * *

Unlike salesmen, partsmen, and mechanics, service advisors "wor[k] ordinary, fixed schedules on-site." Respondents, for instance, work *regular* 11-hour shifts, at all times of the year, for a weekly minimum of 55 hours. Service advisors thus do not implicate the concerns underlying the § 213(b)(10)(A) exemption. Indeed, they are precisely the type of workers Congress intended the FLSA to shield "from the evil of overwork."

* * *

Petitioner contends that "affirming the decision below would disrupt decades of settled expectations" while exposing "employers to substantial retroactive liability." "[M]any dealerships," petitioner urges, "have offered compensation packages based primarily on sales commissions," in reliance on court decisions and agency guidance ranking service advisors as exempt.

Congress . . . has spoken directly to the treatment of *commission-based* workers. The FLSA exempts from its overtime directives any employee of a "retail or service establishment" who receives more than half of his or her pay on commission, so long as the employee's "regular rate of pay" is more than 1 ½ times the minimum wage. § 207(i). Thus, even without the § 213(b)(10)(A) exemption, many service advisors compensated on commission would remain ineligible for overtime remuneration.

In crafting the commission-pay exemption, Congress struck a deliberate balance: It exempted *higher* paid commissioned employees, perhaps in recognition of their potentially irregular hours, but it maintained protection for *lower* paid employees, to vindicate the Act's "principal . . . purpose" of shielding "workers from substandard wages and oppressive working hours."

This Court once recognized that the "particularity" of FLSA exemptions "preclude[s] their enlargement by implication." . . . The Court today, in adding an exemption of its own creation, veers away from that comprehension of the FLSA's mission.

Page 461. Please add to the end of the first paragraph.

The Trump Administration has not continued to pursue this initiative. Shortly after Secretary of Labor Alex Acosta was confirmed, he withdrew the an Obama-era Administrator Interpretation entitled *The Application of the Fair Labor Standards Act's 'Suffer or Permit' Standard in the Identification of Employees Who Are Misclassified as Independent Contractors*, which had sought to define relatively broadly the scope of "employee" under the FLSA.

Page 462. Please add at end of Note 1.

On May 18, 2016, the Department of Labor announced a raise in the salary threshold for mandatory overtime pay from $23,660 to $47,476. The rule was blocked by a U.S. District Court. Nevada v. United States Department of Labor, 218 F.Supp.3d 520 (E.D. Tex. 2016). The Trump Administration filed an appeal, which was stayed as of June 2018 while the Administration pursues a new rulemaking. That rulemaking is expected to set the threshold somewhere above $23,660, but below $47,476.

Page 465. Please add to Note 5.

Beginning in 1975, the Department of Labor's interpretation of the statutory exemption from FLSA protections for certain "domestic service" workers included caretakers employed by third-party agencies. In 2013 the DOL changed its interpretation to restrict the exemption to workers hired directly by the home care recipients and their families. Held: The DOL's change in the law's coverage is reasonable and therefore within its authority. Home Care Ass'n of America v. Weil, 799 F.3d 1084 (D.C. Cir. 2015), cert. denied, 136 S.Ct. 2506 (2016).

Page 465. Please add notes.

7. Exotic dancers are employees and not independent contractors. McFeeley v. Jackson Street Entertainment, LLC, 825 F.3d 235 (4th Cir. 2016).

8. An interesting dispute is whether minor league baseball players should be covered by the FLSA or whether they are "professionals." See Senne v. Office of the Comm'r of Baseball, 315 F.R.D. 523 (N.D. Cal. 2016) (decertifying class). See Lucas J. Carney, Major League Baseball's 'Foul Ball': Why Minor League Baseball Players are Not Exempt Employees under the Fair Labor Standards Act, 41 J. Corp. L. 283 (2015).

Page 465. Please insert before d. Wages.

Lola v. Skadden, Arps, Slate, Meagher & Flom
620 Fed. Appx. 37 (2d Cir. 2015).

■ POOLER, CIRCUIT JUDGE.

David Lola, on behalf of himself and all others similarly situated, appeals from the September 16, 2014 opinion and order of the United States District Court for the Southern District of New York (Sullivan, J.) dismissing his putative collective action seeking damages from Skadden, Arps, Slate, Meagher & Flom LLP and Tower Legal Staffing, Inc. for violations of the overtime provision of the Fair Labor Standards Act, 29 U.S.C. §§ 201 et seq. ("FLSA"), arising out of Lola's work as a contract attorney in North Carolina. We agree with the district court's conclusion that: (1) state, not federal, law informs FLSA's definition of "practice of law;" and (2) North Carolina, as the place where Lola worked and lived, has the greatest interest in this litigation, and thus we look to North Carolina law to determine if Lola was practicing law within the meaning of FLSA. However, we disagree with the district court's conclusion, on a motion to dismiss, that by undertaking the document review Lola allegedly was hired to conduct, Lola was necessarily "practicing law" within the meaning of North Carolina law. We find that accepting the allegations as pleaded, Lola adequately alleged in his complaint that his document review was devoid of legal judgment such that he was not engaged in the practice of law, and remand for further proceedings.

* * *

Lola, a North Carolina resident, alleges that beginning in April 2012, he worked for Defendants for fifteen months in North Carolina. He conducted document review for Skadden in connection with a multi-district litigation pending in the United States District Court for the Northern District of Ohio. Lola is an attorney licensed to practice law in California, but he is not admitted to practice law in either North Carolina or the Northern District of Ohio.

Lola alleges that his work was closely supervised by the Defendants, and his "entire responsibility . . . consisted of (a) looking at documents to see what search terms, if any, appeared in the documents, (b) marking those documents into the categories predetermined by Defendants, and (c) at times drawing black boxes to redact portions of certain documents based on specific protocols that Defendants provided." Lola further alleges that Defendants provided him with the documents he reviewed, the search terms he was to use in connection with those documents, and the procedures he was to follow if the search terms appeared. Lola was paid $25 an hour for his work, and worked roughly forty-five to fifty-five hours a week. He was paid at the same rate for any hours he worked in excess of forty hours per week. Lola was told that he was an employee of Tower, but he was also told that he needed to follow any procedures set by Skadden attorneys, and he worked under the supervision of Skadden attorneys. Other attorneys employed to work on the same project performed similar work and were likewise paid hourly rates that remained the same for any hours worked in excess of forty hours per week.

* * *

Pursuant to FLSA, employers must generally pay employees working overtime one and one-half times the regular rate of pay for any hours worked in excess of forty a week. However, employees "employed in a bona fide . . . professional capacity" are exempt from that requirement. The statute does not provide a definition of "professional capacity," instead delegating the authority to do so to the Secretary of the Department of Labor ("DOL"), who defines "professional employees" to include those employees who are:

(1) Compensated on a salary or fee basis at a rate of not less than $455 per week . . .; and

(2) Whose primary duty is the performance of work:

    (i) Requiring knowledge of an advanced type in a field of science or learning customarily acquired by a prolonged course of intellectual instruction; or

    (ii) Requiring invention, imagination, originality or talent in a recognized field of artistic or creative endeavor.

These requirements, however, do not apply to attorneys engaged in the practice of law. Instead, attorneys fall under 29 C.F.R. § 541.304, which exempts from the overtime requirement:

Any employee who is the holder of a valid license or certificate permitting the practice of law or medicine or any of their branches and is actually engaged in the practice thereof[.]

While it is undisputed that Lola is an attorney licensed to practice law in California, the parties dispute whether the document review he allegedly performed constitutes "engaging in the practice of law."

Lola urges us to fashion a new federal standard defining the "practice of law" within the meaning of Section 541.304. We decline to do so because we agree with the district court that the definition of "practice of law" is "primarily a matter of state concern."

* * *

Just as "there is no federal law of domestic relations," here there is no federal law governing lawyers. Regulating the "practice of law" is traditionally a state endeavor. No federal scheme exists for issuing law licenses. As the district court aptly observed, "[s]tates regulate almost every aspect of legal practice: they set the eligibility criteria and oversee the admission process for would-be lawyers, promulgate the rules of professional ethics, and discipline lawyers who fail to follow those rules, among many other responsibilities." The exemption in FLSA specifically relies on the attorney possessing "a valid license . . . permitting the practice of law." The regulation's history indicates that the DOL was well aware that such licenses were issued by the states. In rejecting a proposal to exempt librarians from the overtime rules, the DOL noted that "states do not generally license the practice of library science, so that in this respect . . . the profession is not comparable to that of law or medicine." A similar distinction was drawn in a discussion of extending the exemption to architects and engineers:

> The practice of law and medicine has a long history of state licensing and certification; the licensing of engineers and architects is relatively recent. While it is impossible for a doctor or lawyer legally to practice his profession without a certificate or license, many architects and engineers perform work in these fields without possessing licenses, although failure to hold a license may limit their permissible activities to those of lesser responsibilities.

We thus find no error with the district court's conclusion that we should look to state law in defining the "practice of law."

We turn to the question of which state's law to apply. "Where jurisdiction is based on the existence of a federal question . . . we have not hesitated to apply a federal common law choice of law analysis." * * * Here, there are four possible forum states: North Carolina (where Lola worked and lived); Ohio (where the underlying litigation is venued); California (where Lola is barred); and New York (where Skadden is located).

* * *

Here, the services were rendered in North Carolina. Moreover, as the state where Lola resides, North Carolina possesses a strong interest in making sure Lola is fairly paid. We find no error in the district court's decision to apply North Carolina law.

North Carolina defines the "practice of law" in its General Statutes, Section 84–2.1, which provides that:

The phrase "practice law" as used in this Chapter is defined to be performing any legal service for any other person, firm or corporation, with or without compensation, specifically including . . . the preparation and filing of petitions for use in any court, including administrative tribunals and other judicial or quasi-judicial bodies, or assisting by advice, counsel, or otherwise in any legal work; and to advise or give opinion upon the legal rights of any person, firm or corporation . . . .

North Carolina courts typically read Section 84–2.1 in conjunction with Section 84–4, which defines the unauthorized practice of law as follows:

Except as otherwise permitted by law, . . . it shall be unlawful for any person or association of persons except active members of the Bar, for or without a fee or consideration, to give legal advice or counsel, [or] perform for or furnish to another legal services . . . .

The North Carolina General Statutes do not clarify whether "legal services" includes the performance of document review. Nevertheless, the North Carolina State Bar issued a formal ethics opinion shedding light on what is meant by "legal services." The question considered in the ethics opinion was: "May a lawyer ethically outsource legal support services abroad, if the individual providing the services is either a nonlawyer or a lawyer not admitted to practice in the United States (collectively 'foreign assistants')?" In its opinion, the Bar's Ethics Committee opined that:

A lawyer may use foreign assistants for administrative support services such as document assembly, accounting, and clerical support. A lawyer may also use foreign assistants for limited legal support services such as reviewing documents; conducting due diligence; drafting contracts, pleadings, and memoranda of law; and conducting legal research. Foreign assistants may not exercise independent legal judgment in making decisions on behalf of a client. . . . The limitations on the type of legal services that can be outsourced, in conjunction with the selection and supervisory requirements associated with the use of foreign assistants, insures that the client is competently represented. *See* Rule 5.5(d). Nevertheless, when outsourcing legal support services, lawyers need to be mindful of the prohibitions on unauthorized practice of law in Chapter 84 of the General Statutes and on the prohibition on aiding the unauthorized practice of law in Rule 5.5(d).

The district court found that (1) under North Carolina law, document review is considered "legal support services," along with "drafting contracts, pleadings, and memoranda of law[,] and conducting legal research;" (2) the ethics opinion draws a clear line between legal support services, like document review, and "administrative support services," like "document assembly, accounting, and clerical support;" and (3) by emphasizing that only lawyers may undertake legal work, the ethics opinion makes clear that "document review, like other legal support services, constitutes the practice of law and may be lawfully performed by a non-lawyer only if that non-lawyer is supervised by a licensed attorney." Thus, the district court concluded, any level of document review is considered the "practice of law" in North Carolina. The district court also concluded that because FLSA's regulatory scheme carves doctors and lawyers out of the salary and duty analysis employed to discern if other types of employees fall within the professional exemption, a fact-intensive inquiry is at odds with FLSA's regulatory scheme.

We disagree. The district court erred in concluding that engaging in document review per se constitutes practicing law in North Carolina. The ethics opinion does not delve into precisely what type of document review falls within the practice of law, but does note that while "reviewing documents" may be within the practice of law, "[f]oreign assistants may not exercise independent legal judgment in making decisions on behalf of a client." The ethics opinion strongly suggests that inherent in the definition of "practice of law" in North Carolina is the exercise of at least a modicum of independent legal judgment.

* * *

The gravamen of Lola's complaint is that he performed document review under such tight constraints that he exercised no legal judgment whatsoever—he alleges that he used criteria developed by others to simply sort documents into different categories. Accepting those allegations as true, as we must on a motion to dismiss, we find that Lola adequately alleged in his complaint that he failed to exercise any legal judgment in performing his duties for Defendants. A fair reading of the complaint in the light most favorable to Lola is that he provided services that a machine could have provided. The parties themselves agreed at oral argument that an individual who, in the course of reviewing discovery documents, undertakes tasks that could otherwise be performed entirely by a machine cannot be said to engage in the practice of law. We therefore vacate the judgment of the district court and remand for further proceedings consistent with this opinion.

NOTE

The plaintiffs and Skadden, Arps settled the *Lola* lawsuit and the U.S. District Judge approved the settlement. Lola v. Skadden, Arps, Slate, Meagher & Flom LLP, 2016 WL 922223 (S.D.N.Y. 2016).

d.   WAGES

Page 467. Please add to Note 8.

If a restaurant is paying legal minimum wage or more to both servers and kitchen employees, can it require "tips" received by servers to be shared with both groups of workers? The legal question is whether an Obama Administration Department of Labor regulation saying that servers should get all the tip money is an invalid extension of the FLSA. The regulation was upheld by the Ninth Circuit in Oregon Restaurant & Lodging Ass'n v. Perez, 816 F.3d 1080 (9th Cir. 2017). However, the Tenth Circuit reached the opposite conclusion. Marlow v. New Food Guy, 861 F.3d 1157 (10th Cir. 2017) (employee who made above the minimum wage was not entitled to tips under FLSA, and DOL did not have the authority to promulgate a rule to the contrary).

Another issue involving tips concerns when an employee who performs some tipped work and some non-tipped work is entitled to be paid the full minimum wage for the time spent doing the non-tipped work. In Marsh v. J. Alexander's, the court wrote that an employee did not have "dual jobs" (which would trigger the employer's obligation to pay the minimum wage for the employee's time spent performing the non-tipped job) based on the fact that he had to perform intermittent tasks such as cleaning or making tea during the course of a restaurant server job. In reaching that conclusion, the court refused to defer to the DOL's interpretation of its dual jobs regulation. 869 F.3d 1108 (9th Cir. 2017) (rehearing en banc granted).

Page 467. Please add a new Note 9.

9.   The Los Angeles Living Wage Ordinance requires contractors who operate at the city's airports to pay their employees $14.89 per hour or $10.30 per hour if the contractor provides health benefits. See Calop Bus. Sys., Inc. v. City of Los Angeles, 614 Fed. Appx. 867 (9th Cir. 2015).

Seattle raised minimum wages more for large employers and classified certain franchisees as large employers. The new policy survived legal challenges. International Franchise Ass'n v. City of Seattle, 803 F.3d 389 (9th Cir. 2015), cert. denied, 136 S.Ct. 1838 (2016).

Efforts by cities to raise the minimum wage are not always successful, however. In at least seventeen states, state legislatures have prohibited localities from enacting minimum wage ordinances. The most recent state to do so was Alabama. In April 2015, the Birmingham City Council adopted a series of ordinances enacting a local minimum wage. Shortly thereafter, the Alabama state legislature passed the Alabama Uniform Minimum Wage and Right-to-Work Act. Ala. Code §§ 25–7–40 (2016). An effort to increase state uniformity in labor policy, the Act gave the legislature complete control over minimum wage policy and a host of other labor policy issues. The plaintiffs brought suit in district court, alleging that the Act has the effect of transferring control over minimum wages in the City of Birmingham from officials elected by a majority-black electorate to legislators elected by a majority-white electorate, and therefore violates protections under Section 2 of the Voting Rights Act, and the Thirteenth, Fourteenth, and Fifteenth

Amendments. The court upheld the defendants' motion to dismiss, finding that the plaintiffs (1) lacked standing by suing the wrong defendants, (2) failed to state a claim under Section 2 of the Voting Rights Act, (3) raised Section 2 claims that were barred by the Eleventh Amendment, (4) failed to plausibly plea an equal protection claim, and (5) were not entitled to go forward on their race discrimination claims. Lewis v. Bentley, 2017 WL 432464 (N.D. Ala., 2017). However, the plaintiffs appealed to the 11th Circuit, which reversed in part and remanded to the district court. That Court held that that plaintiffs had stated a plausible equal protection claim, which requires them to show that the state preemption law has a racially discriminatory impact, and was enacted with an intent to discriminate based on race. Lewis v. Governor of Alabama, ___ F.3d ___, 2018 WL 3552408 (11th Cir. 2018).

e.   HOURS

Page 473. Please add to Note 1.

California law requires employers to permit their employees to take off-duty rest periods. The California Supreme Court decided that employers may not require employees to remain "on call" during these rest periods. Thus, ABM Security Services cannot require guards to keep their pagers and radio phones on during rest periods and to "remain vigilant and responsive to calls when needs arose." Augustus v. ABM Security Services, Inc., 347 P.3d 89 (Cal. 2016) (5–2).

Page 473. Please add to Note 2.

In Department of Labor v. American Future Systems, 873 F.3d 420 (3d Cir. 2017) the Third Circuit held that employers were required to compensate employees for breaks of twenty minutes or fewer.

Page 476. Please add to the end of Note 12.

The Supreme Court reversed, holding that by enacting the Portal-to-Portal Act, Congress cut back on the broad judicial interpretation given to the FLSA's undefined terms "work" and "workweek." The Court unanimously held that employers do not have to pay for "activities which are preliminary to or postliminary to" the principal activities that an employee is hired to perform. Integrity Staffing Solutions, Inc. v. Busk, 135 S.Ct. 513 (2014).

Page 476. Please insert as new notes.

13. In 1999 and 2001, the Department of Labor said that mortgage-loan officers are not administrators exempt from overtime pay requirements. In 2006, the Department said they were exempt as administrators. In 2010, the Department withdrew the 2006 letter and restored overtime pay to them. The Mortgage Bankers Association sued, arguing that the 2010 action did not meet the procedural requirements of the Administrative Procedure Act. The Supreme Court said the Department's 2010 action did satisfy the APA. Perez v. Mortgage Bankers Ass'n, 135 S.Ct. 1199 (2015).

Should the hours worked by employees employed by two companies be aggregated for the purposes of the FLSA? The pivotal question to answer in such cases is whether the employees are jointly or separately employed. An employer of a separately employed employee can disregard the work the employee performs for the other employer. If the employee is jointly employed, however, then the work the employee performs for both employers is aggregated when determining compliance of both employers with the FLSA. 29 C.F.R. § 791.2 (1961).

The Fourth Circuit recently took up this issue in Salinas v. Commercial Interiors, Inc. 848 F.3d 125 (4th Cir. 2017). There, a host of plaintiffs employed as dry wall installers for both J.I., a dry wall installation subcontractor, and Commercial, a general contracting company, sued the two companies, arguing that the hours they worked for both companies be aggregated to assess the companies' compliance with the FLSA. The district court granted summary judgment to Commercial, finding that joint employment did not exist because the agreement entered into between the two companies was a traditionally recognized contractor-subcontractor relationship, and the companies did not intent to avoid compliance with the FLSA. The Fourth Circuit reversed and remanded, holding:

> Joint employment exists when (1) two or more persons or entities share, agree to allocate responsibility for, or otherwise codetermine—formally or informally, directly or indirectly—the essential terms and conditions of a worker's employment and (2) the two entities' combined influence over the essential terms and conditions of the worker's employment render the worker an employee as opposed to an independent contractor. 848 F.3d at 130.

Applying this test, the court found that the undisputed facts in the case established that the J.I. and Commercial shared authority over and codetermined the terms and conditions of the plaintiffs' employment. Commercial actively supervised the work of J.I.'s employees, provided all the tools needed for the work, coordinated staffing hours and pay with J.I., and, on at least one occasion, required J.I. employees to apply for employment with Commercial. The court affirmed the district court's finding that the plaintiffs were employees and not independent contractors using the economic realities test.

14. A group of Tyson Foods employees brought a class action against the company, asserting that their FLSA rights were violated when Tyson failed to provide overtime compensation for donning and doffing protective equipment and clothing before work, before and after lunch, and at the end of the workday. The Supreme Court affirmed a $5.7 million jury verdict for the class, concluding that statistical evidence derived from studying a sample of the plaintiffs was an adequate basis for the class action. The Court was influenced by the fact that the employer had not kept records adequate for challenging the plaintiffs' sample evidence. The employees had done similar work and were paid under the same policy, a reason for distinguishing this case from Wal-Mart Stores, Inc. v. Dukes, p. 226. The Supreme Court affirmed a jury verdict of $5.7 million for the class. Chief Justice Roberts, joined by Justice Alito, concurred but expressed his "concern that the District Court may not be able to fashion a method for awarding damages only to those class members who suffered an actual injury." Tyson Foods, Inc. v. Bouaphakeo, 136 S.Ct. 1036 (2016) (6–2).

g.   ENFORCEMENT OF THE FLSA

Page 486. Please replace Note 6 with the following.

6.   Does a lawsuit become moot when one party (usually the defendant) offers to pay everything the plaintiff requested? Compare Genesis Healthcare Corp. v. Symczyk, 133 S.Ct. 1523 (2013)(5–4), an FLSA case, with Campbell-Ewald Co. v. Gomez, 136 S.Ct. 663 (2016)(6–3), not an employment law case. The two cases found different reasons for concluding that the plaintiff's case was not mooted.

B.   WHAT IS A JOB WORTH?

2.   WAGE COMPARABILITY FOR INDIVIDUALS: THE QUEST FOR PAY EQUITY

Page 500. Please insert both a "Note" heading and this note above a. The Equal Pay Act.

Figures from the Bureau of Labor Statistics for 2015 show that the median weekly earnings for full-time wage and salary workers were: $920 for white males; $680 for black males; $1,129 for Asian males; $631 for Hispanic males; $743 for white females; $615 for black females; $877 for Asian females; $566 for Hispanic females. Bureau of Labor Statistics, Highlights of Women's Earnings in 2015 (2016). On average, women who work full-time earn roughly 81% of what their male counterparts earn.

According to a Pew Research Center analysis, while wage disparity by gender has shrunk from 36 cents on the dollar in 1980 to 17 cents in 2015, certain groups have seen notable differences. For young women ages 25–34, the wage gap with young men has decreased from 37 cents in 1980 to 10 cents in 2015. By race, the disparity is also striking. Compared to white males, the wage gap between 1980 and 2015 among white women decreased by 22 cents; for black women, 9 cents; for Asian women, the records only start after 1980 but are approximately the same as for white women; for Hispanic women, 5 cents. Pew Research Center tabulations of Current Population Survey data, 2015.

a.   THE EQUAL PAY ACT

Page 504. Please insert the following case above the Notes and Questions.

Rizo v. Yovino

887 F.3d 453 (9th Cir. 2018) (en banc).

■ REINHARDT, CIRCUIT JUDGE:

The Equal Pay Act stands for a principle as simple as it is just: men and women should receive equal pay for equal work regardless of sex. The question before us is also simple: can an employer justify a wage differential between male and female employees by relying on prior salary? Based on the text, history, and purpose of the Equal Pay Act, the answer is clear: No. Congress recognized in 1963 that the Equal Pay Act was long overdue: "Justice and fairplay speak so eloquently [on] behalf of the equal pay for women bill that it seems unnecessary to belabor the point. We can only marvel that it has taken us so long to recognize the fact that equity and economic soundness support this legislation." Salaries speak louder than words, however. Although the Act has prohibited sex-based wage discrimination for more than fifty years, the financial exploitation of working women embodied by the gender pay gap continues to be an embarrassing reality of our economy.

Prior to this decision, our law was unclear whether an employer could consider prior salary, either alone or in combination with other factors, when setting its employees' salaries. We took this case *en banc* in order to clarify the law, and we now hold that prior salary alone or in combination with other factors cannot justify a wage differential. To hold otherwise—to allow employers to capitalize on the persistence of the wage gap and perpetuate that gap *ad infinitum*—would be contrary to the text and history of the Equal Pay Act, and would vitiate the very purpose for which the Act stands.

Fresno County Office of Education ("the County") does not dispute that it pays Aileen Rizo ("Rizo") less than comparable male employees for the same work. . . . The County contends that that the wage differential is based on the [Equal Pay Act's] fourth exception—the catchall exception: a "factor other than sex." . . . Because we conclude that prior salary does not constitute a "factor than sex," the County fails as a matter of law to set forth an affirmative defense.

* * *

The Equal Pay Act "creates a type of strict liability" for employers who pay men and women different wages for the same work: once a plaintiff demonstrates a wage disparity, she is *not* required to prove discriminatory intent. . . .

The question in this case is the meaning of the catchall exception. This is purely a question of law. We conclude, unhesitatingly, that "any other factor other than sex" is limited to legitimate, job-related factors such as a prospective employee's experience, educational background, ability, or prior job performance. It is inconceivable that Congress, in an Act the primary purpose of which was to eliminate long-existing "endemic" sex-based wage disparities, would create an exception for basing new hires' salaries on those very disparities—disparities that Congress declared are not only related to sex but caused by sex. To accept the County's argument would be to perpetuate rather than eliminate the pervasive discrimination at which the Act was aimed. As explained later in this opinion, the language, legislative history, and purpose of the Act make it clear that Congress was not so benighted. Prior salary, whether considered alone or with other factors, is not job related and thus does not fall within an exception to the Act that allows employers to pay disparate wages. Reflecting the very essence of the Act, we hold that by relying on prior salary, the County fails as a matter of law to set forth an affirmative defense.

* * *

Basic principles of statutory interpretation also establish that prior salary is not a permissible "factor other than sex" within the meaning of the Equal Pay Act. The County maintains that the catchall exception unambiguously provides that any facially neutral factor constitutes an affirmative defense to liability under the Equal Pay Act. It is incorrect. . . . [It] is clear that when the catchall exception is read in light of its surrounding context and legislative history, a legitimate "factor other than sex" must be job related and that prior salary cannot justify paying one gender less if equal work is performed.

Where, as here, a statute contains a catchall term at the end of a list, we rely on the related principles of *noscitur a sociis* and *ejusdem generis* to "cabin the contextual meaning" of the term, and to "avoid ascribing to [that term] a meaning so broad that it is inconsistent with its accompanying words, thus giving unintended breadth to the Acts of Congress."

The canon *noscitur a sociis*—"a word is known by the company it keeps"—provides that words grouped together should be given related meaning. Here, the catchall phrase is grouped with three specific exceptions based on systems of seniority, merit, and productivity. These specific systems share more in common than mere gender neutrality; all three relate to job qualifications, performance, and/or experience. It follows that the more general exception should be limited to legitimate, job-related reasons as well.

A related canon, *ejusdem generis*, likewise supports our interpretation of the catchall term. We apply this canon when interpreting general terms at the end of a list of more specific ones. In such a case, "the general words are construed to embrace only objects similar in nature to those objects enumerated by the preceding specific words." The inclusion of the word "other" before the general provision in the Equal Pay Act makes its meaning all the more clear: "[T]he principle of *ejusdem generis* . . . implies the addition of *similar* after the word *other*." Antonin Scalia & Bryan A. Garner, Reading Law: The Interpretation of Legal Texts 199 (2012). Here, we read the statutory exceptions as: "(i) a seniority system, (ii) a merit system, (iii) a system which measures earnings by quantity or quality of production; or (iv) a differential based on any other [*similar*] factor other than sex." 29 U.S.C. § 206(d)(1). A similar factor would have to be one similar to the other legitimate, job-related reasons. . . .

We, too, look to the history of the legislative process and draw a similar conclusion that the inclusion of the catchall provision in the final bill was in direct response to the entreaties of industry witnesses. Industry representatives testified at the congressional subcommittee hearings that the two exceptions in the bills that had been introduced in the House and Senate were too specific and under inclusive, and "evidence[d] . . . a lack of understanding of industrial reality." The witnesses were concerned that companies would no longer be able to rely on the wide variety of factors used across industries to measure the value of a particular job. Accordingly, the witnesses proposed a series of job-related exceptions in addition to the two original exceptions that had covered only seniority and merit systems.

Chief among those was an exception for job classification programs. The Vice President of Owens-Illinois Glass Co. testified: "Job classification and wage incentive programs are so widely accepted . . . in American industry that there seems little need to set forth a lengthy list of reasons why they should be excepted from the present bill." Id. at 101 (statement of W. Boyd Owen, Vice President of Personnel Administration, Owens-Illinois Glass Co.). Bona fide job classification programs were necessarily job related because they were used to "establish relative job worth" in diverse industries, "each [of which] has its own peculiarities and its own customs." Id. at 238 (statement of E.G. Hester, Director of Industrial Relations Research, Corning Glass Works). Using factors like skill and responsibility, these classification programs were "a yardstick against which [employers] can measure work performance and consequently pay." Id. at 146 (statement of John G. Wayman, Partner, Reed, Smith, Shaw & McClay). The Owens-Illinois Glass representative, Mr. Owen, explained that his proposed exceptions based on job classification and wage incentive programs would "merely parallel" the existing exceptions for seniority and merit systems, id. at 101, both of which were themselves job related. . . .

We think it plain that the catchall exception was added to the final Equal Pay Act in direct response to these employers' concerns that their legitimate, job-related means of setting pay would not be covered under the two exceptions already included in the bill.

* * *

Prior salary does not fit within the catchall exception because it is not a legitimate measure of work experience, ability, performance, or any other job-related quality. It may bear a rough relationship to legitimate factors other than sex, such as training, education, ability, or experience, but the relationship is attenuated. More important, it may well operate to perpetuate the wage disparities prohibited under the Act. Rather than use a second-rate surrogate that likely masks continuing inequities, the employer must instead point directly to the underlying factors for which prior salary is a rough proxy, at best, if it is to prove its wage differential is justified under the catchall exception.

* * *

[Concurring opinions omitted]

Page 508. Please add a new note after Note 7 and renumber Note 8 as Note 9.

8.   As noted in Chapter 3, some cities have barred employers from asking about job candidates' prior salaries. One of these laws has been challenged under the First Amendment.

c.   THE LILLY LEDBETTER FAIR PAY ACT

Page 533. Please add both a "Note" heading and the following note.

A new California law prohibits employers from paying different wages to employees who do "substantially similar work." The law also prohibits retaliation against employees who inquire about their colleagues' salaries. The California law is a version of the Paycheck Fairness Act that the U.S. Congress declined to enact in 2014. Cal. Lab. Code § 1197.5 (2016).

In 2016, Massachusetts became the first state to amend their equal pay laws by prohibiting employers from inquiring about an applicant's current or previous salary. In 2017, Philadelphia became the first city to implement laws with similar prohibitions, followed by the city of New York. The Massachusetts amendment also follows several other states in providing employees the right to discuss their salary with other employees, free from retaliation by the employer. Additionally, Massachusetts has struck out any definition of "Woman" (previously "a female 18 or older"), and uses the term "gender" in regard to pay discrimination, with no mention of "male" or "female." While some states' equal pay acts continue to prohibit wage discrepancy between men and women, or to include phrases such as "the opposite gender," the use of non-binary terms has increased as further laws are being passed.

CHAPTER 6

HEALTH BENEFITS

A. INTRODUCTION

Page 543. Please add the following new section under Individual Responsibility.

Concurrent with the employer's obligations under the ACA, beginning in 2014, individuals were required to maintain minimal essential health care coverage for themselves and their dependents. Individuals who failed to maintain such coverage were subject to a penalty to be included in their tax return. The penalty was to be either a percentage of the individual's household income, or a flat dollar amount for each year the individual failed to maintain coverage, whichever is greater.

This so-called "individual mandate" exempted certain individuals from coverage, including individuals who object to health care coverage on religious grounds, who were not lawfully present in the United States, or who were incarcerated. The law also provided exceptions to the penalty for certain low income individuals, including individuals who could not afford coverage and individuals whose income was less than 100% of the federal poverty level, members of Indian tribes, and individuals who suffered hardship.

Congress completely repealed the individual mandate of the ACA as part of a comprehensive tax reform package in December 2017, and which will go into effect January 1, 2019. It is unclear, at this time, how significant an impact this loss of members from the health insurance risk pool will have on the overall working of the ACA or how many more people will now end up without health insurance. The Congressional Budget Office has predicted that the loss of the individual mandate will lead to 4 million people deciding to forgo insurance in 2019 and 13 million people dropping coverage by 2027. Another possible consequence is that the repeal will raise healthcare insurance premiums and cause the ACA's health insurance exchanges (discussed below) to fall part.

Page 544. Please delete the bullet point on the Individual Mandate.

Page 544. Please add the following new sentences to the bullet point on the High Cost Plan Excise Tax.

On January 22, 2018, Congress passed a temporary funding bill (until February 8, 2018), which continued funding federal government activity, changed the effective date for the 40% excise tax on high-cost health care until 2022. The so-called "Cadillac Tax" was originally scheduled to become effective in 2018, but in 2015 it was delayed until 2020. At a minimum, the new two-year delay gives employers and plan sponsors more time to adjust health plan design to avoid the Cadillac Tax.

Page 544. Please add the following new bullet point on Association Health Plans.

• *Association Health Plans (AHPs).* On June 21, 2018, the U.S. Department of Labor released a final rule, "Definition of 'Employer' Under Section 3(5) of ERISA—Association Health Plans," 83 Fed. Reg. 28912 (June 21, 2018). The AHP Final Rule expands the universe of arrangements that can qualify as an AHP for purposes of ERISA and also applies large group treatment to qualifying AHP coverage. The AHP Final Rule achieves this by broadening the criteria under ERISA for determining when employers may join together in an association that is treated as the ERISA "employer" of a single group health plan and by allowing certain self-employed persons to be treated as employers under appropriate circumstances.

Page 545. Please add the following as the third paragraph on the page.

Another Supreme Court case challenging the legality of the ACA is King v. Burwell, 135 S.Ct. 2480 (2015). The plaintiffs lived in Virginia, a state that has not created a state exchange and whose residents therefore used the federal exchange to purchase individual health insurance. The plaintiffs argued that there was no statutory basis for the IRS to give tax credits for use on the federal exchange because Section 36B of the ACA only describes tax credits for exchanges "established by the State." The Supreme Court, 6–3, rejected the plaintiffs' argument. In an opinion by Chief Justice Roberts, the Court held that the challenged portion of the text needs to be considered in light of the ACA's context and structure. The majority noted that the lack of a state *and* federal exchange in any state would deny tax credits and health coverage, thereby threatening the basic goals of the law.

> Congress passed the Affordable Care Act to improve health insurance markets, not to destroy them. If at all possible, we must interpret the Act in a way that is consistent with the former, and avoids the latter. Section 36B can fairly be read consistent with what we see as Congress's plan, and that is the reading we adopt.

135 S.Ct. at 2496. In a characteristically animated dissent, Justice Scalia wrote:

> The Act that Congress passed makes tax credits available only on an "Exchange established by the State." This Court, however, concludes that this limitation would prevent the rest of the Act from working as well as hoped. So it rewrites the law to make tax credits available everywhere. We should start calling this law SCOTUScare.

135 S.Ct. at 2506.

In Zubik v. Burwell, 136 S.Ct. 444 (2016), nonprofit organizations that provide health insurance to their employees challenged a regulation promulgated to implement the ACA requiring them to provide certain contraceptive services as part of their health plans unless they submit a form either to their insurer or to the federal government indicating that they object on religious grounds. The organizations alleged that submitting the notice substantially burdens the exercise of their religion in violation of the Religious Freedom Restoration Act of 1993, 42 U.S.C. § 2000bb et seq. In a per curiam opinion, the Court vacated decisions of the lower courts and remanded the case to allow the parties to resolve the issues themselves. Many commentators believed that this action was to avoid a four-to-four split by the justices caused by the death of Justice Scalia.

Page 545. Please add the following as the fourth paragraph on the page.

Although not technically an employee benefits case, the public accommodations case, *Masterpiece Cake v. Colorado Civil Rights Commission*, 138 S.Ct. 1719 (2018), may have employment benefit law implications. *Masterpiece Cakeshop* deals with a cake shop owner's claim that his religious freedom should allow him to refuse customers who wanted a cake for a same-sex wedding. The Supreme Court reversed a state commission's decision against the shop owner, holding that the decision violated the cake shop owner's right to free expression. But the decision is narrower than it may first appear. In particular, the Court appeared to hinge the decision on the state commission's decision in the case, which it viewed as being impermissibly hostile to religion (this may have led to the 7–2 lineup at the Court).

The Court seemed to duck the underlying issue about free expression v. antidiscrimination laws. Employers will no doubt try to use *Masterpiece* as a defense. Its value will depend on employers' ability to couch their employment discrimination as expression because one of the unique aspects of *Masterpiece* was that the shop owner claimed that making cakes was artistic—that is, constitutionally protected expression. Because of that, and the Court's criticism of the state anti-discrimination commission, it may be that most employers will not be able to make an argument like *Masterpiece*. There will no doubt be exceptions—maybe a religious-themed artist that hires assistants—but there are not a lot of businesses that involve both the level of expression needed for such a claim, as well as the level of hostility that the Court perceived. So stay tuned to see if *Masterpiece* is not cited in the next significant ERISA same-sex benefits case. The ability of private employers to assert religious or moral objections to providing contraceptive coverage may only be the start of attempts to assert such objections to the provision of other employee benefits. This trend may affect the provision of medical benefits for transgender employees, coverage for same-sex spouses in health plans, fertility benefits for employees in same-sex relationships, and medical marijuana.

Page 546. Please add the following at the bottom of the page.

When employee wellness programs ask for individual and family medical histories they may implicate the ADA and GINA. Provisions of these two laws permit employer-sponsored wellness programs to request medical or genetic information, but only if participation in the programs is voluntary. Under the final rule issued by the EEOC, 81 Fed. Reg. 31126 (2016), employers are able to award an "incentive" of up to 30% of the total cost of self-only coverage or as high as 50% of the total cost of self-only coverage to implement a smoking cessation program. The average cost of a self-only plan in 2015 was $6251 per year. The EEOC rejected the argument that the amount of the "incentive" (or "penalty" for those who refuse to participate), was so high as to be coercive for lower paid employees who, for all practical purposes, have no choice but to submit their health information and that of their spouse.

In January 2018, the U.S. District Court for the District of Columbia vacated the EEOC's wellness rule effective Jan. 1, 2019, instructing the agency that its goal of revising the rule by 2021 was too slow. *AARP v. EEOC*, No. 16-2113 (D.D.C. Dec. 20, 2017).

C. ERISA—PREEMPTION OF STATE ACTIONS

Page 568. Please insert the following notes.

4A. In Montanile v. Bd. of Trustees, 136 S.Ct. 651 (2016), Montanile was seriously injured by a drunk driver, and his ERISA plan paid more than $120,000 for his medical expenses. Montanile sued the drunk driver and obtained a $500,000 settlement. Pursuant to the plan's subrogation clause the plan administrator sued to recover the funds expended for Montanile's care. Because of the delay in asserting the claim, Montanile spent all of the money on "nontraceable items," such as services or food. The Court held that when the participant dissipates the whole settlement on nontraceable items, the fiduciary cannot bring an action to attach the participant's general assets because the suit is not one for "appropriate equitable relief" under ERISA § 502(a)(3). Because it was unclear whether the participant dissipated all of the settlement in this manner, the case was remanded.

4B. Gobeille v. Liberty Mut. Ins. Co., 136 S.Ct. 936 (2016), involved a challenge to a Vermont law requiring health insurers to report health care claims and other information to a state agency for compilation in an all-inclusive health care database. These "all-payer claims databases" have been enacted in 18 states, and they attempt to generate data on the cost and effectiveness of health care. The Supreme Court held that the Vermont law was preempted by ERISA because ERISA requires plans to file detailed reports with the Secretary of Labor (although different data than required by Vermont) and therefore reporting is a fundamental ERISA function. "Any difference in purpose does not transform this direct regulation of a 'central matter of plan administration,' into an innocuous and peripheral set of additional rules." 136 S.Ct. at 940.

4C. In Coventry Health Care of Missouri, Inc. v. Nevils, 137 S.Ct. 1190 (2017), Jody Nevils, a federal employee, was insured under a health plan pursuant to the Federal Employees Health Benefits Act (FEHBA). Nevils was injured in an auto accident and Coventry paid his medical expenses. After Nevil obtained a settlement against the driver of the other car, Coventry asserted a lien against part of the settlement. Nevils satisfied the lien and then sued in Missouri state court asserting that the lien violated Missouri law. The Missouri Supreme Court held that Missouri law applied and prohibited the lien, but the Supreme Court reversed, holding that the Missouri law was preempted. The Court noted that the preemption language in the FEHBA, prohibiting contractual provisions for subrogation that "relate to" benefits, is the same language that has been broadly construed to require preemption under ERISA.

D. FAMILY AND MEDICAL LEAVE

Page 581. Please change "serious illness" to "serious health condition" in first sentence of Note 4 and add the following cite to beginning of Note 4 string cite.

Pollard v. NY Methodist Hospital, 861 F.3d 374 (2d Cir. 2017) (finding genuine issue of material fact existed precluding summary judgment as to whether employee's foot growth was serious health condition requiring multiple treatments).

Page 582. Please add the following cite to the end of Note 6.

But see Pollard v. NY Methodist Hospital, 861 F.3d 374 (2d Cir. 2017) (holding that state agency's finding in awarding unemployment insurance benefits to former employee that employee provided notice to former employer of surgery "as soon as was practicable" did not preclude employer from challenging whether employee provided adequate notice of her request for FMLA leave).

Page 582. Please add the following note.

6A. In Coutard v. Municipal Credit Union, 848 F.3d 102 (2d Cir. 2017), the plaintiff alleged that his employer violated the FMLA by refusing to permit him to take leave to care for his seriously ill grandfather, who, in loco parentis, had raised him as a child. The FMLA provides for leave under these circumstances, but in requesting leave the plaintiff did not specifically mention the loco parentis relationship. The Second Circuit held that when the employee requested leave, the employer had an obligation to specific any additional information it needed to determine whether the employee was eligible for leave.

Page 582. Please add the following to Note 7.

Accord, Capps v. Mendelez Global, LLC, 847 F.3d 144 (3d Cir. 2017 (applying "honest belief" standard).

Page 584. Please add the following to Note 14.

Additional paid sick leave laws have been enacted in California, Massachusetts, and Oregon. Pursuant to Executive Order 13706 (2015), federal contractors are required to provide up to 7 days annually of paid sick leave.

On June 28, 2018, Massachusetts Governor Baker signed a law affecting all employers in the Commonwealth by creating a paid family and medical leave program funded by a state payroll tax. Beginning in 2021, eligible employees will be allowed to take the following leave in a benefit year: (1) Up to 20 weeks of job-protected paid medical leave to care for their own serious health condition; (2) Up to 12 weeks of job-protected paid family leave to care for a family member with a serious health condition, to bond with the employee's child during the first 12 months after the child's birth or the first 12 months after the placement of the child for adoption or foster care with the employee; and (3) Up to 26 weeks of job-protected paid family leave to care for a covered servicemember. To be eligible for paid family and medical leave, an employee must meet the financial eligibility requirements for receiving unemployment compensation under Massachusetts law.

Page 584. Please add the following notes.

15. Under California law, Cal. Gov't Code § 12945.2, workers are entitled to paid parental leave for six weeks at 55% of their pay, paid for by employee-financed public disability insurance. In 2016, San Francisco enacted a law mandating full pay for parental leave, with the 45% difference being paid by employers. S.F. Police Code art. 33H. New Jersey, N.J. Pub. L. 1948, ch. 110, § 2, and Rhode Island, R.I. Gen. Laws § 28–48, also provide for paid parental leave, but not at full pay, and also financed by employee-funded insurance.

E. NONDISCRIMINATION IN BENEFITS

1. PREGNANCY

Page 588. Please add the following notes.

3. In Young v. United Parcel Service, 135 S.Ct. 1338 (2015) (this supplement at p. 52), the Supreme Court held that a plaintiff could make out a disparate treatment pregnancy discrimination case based on an employer's failure to provide reasonable accommodation when other employees with similar inability to work were accommodated. Although the case did not involve discrimination in benefits, it could well presage a more sympathetic view of the needs of pregnant employees in general, including in the realm of health benefits.

4. On the issue of mandatory coverage of contraceptives, see Burwell v. Hobby Lobby, 134 S.Ct. 2751 (2014) (p. 541 of the main volume).

5. On the issue of possible discrimination in employee benefits in light of religious free exercise rights of employees, see Masterpiece Cake v. Colorado Civil Rights Commission, 138 S.Ct. 1719 (2018) (this supplement at p. 105).

2.   Marital Status

Page 592. Please add the following note before Part 3.

As discussed in the following section, the law of employee health benefits has been changed substantially by striking down state prohibitions on same-sex marriage. In states where same-sex marriage was illegal, some employers extended eligibility for health benefits to domestic partnerships or other non-marital arrangements of same-sex partners, but not opposite-sex partners, on the ground that opposite-sex partners could marry and same-sex partners could not. Now that same-sex marriage is legal in all states, many employers have restructured their benefits to apply to all married couples, but not to any couples in non-marital arrangements. There have been no reported cases as yet by non-marital couples, including by same-sex unmarried couples who lost benefits. Could such a couple argue that if there is a right to marry, there is also a right not to marry, and therefore it is unlawful to deny otherwise available benefits to couples, both same-sex and opposite-sex, that in all other respects are the same as married couples? What arguments, pro and con, would you make in the public sector and the private sector?

3   Sexual Orientation

Page 592. Please delete this entire section and replace with the following text.

In 1996, Congress overwhelmingly enacted, and President Clinton signed, the Defense of Marriage Act (DOMA), which provided that "the word 'marriage' means only a legal union between one man and one woman as husband and wife, and the word 'spouse' refers only to a person of the opposite sex who is a husband or a wife." DOMA § 3. In United States v. Windsor, 133 S.Ct. 2675 (2013), a lawsuit was brought by a surviving same-sex spouse whose inheritance was taxed as if she were unmarried, and thus at a higher rate. The Supreme Court, five-to-four, held that section 3 of DOMA was unconstitutional as a violation of "the liberty of the person protected by the Fifth Amendment."

Later in 2013, the Department of Labor provided guidance to plans, plan sponsors, fiduciaries, participants, and beneficiaries on the Windsor decision's impact on ERISA. According to DOL Technical Release No. 2013-04, generally the terms "spouse" and "marriage" in ERISA include same-sex couples who are legally married in any state or foreign jurisdiction that recognizes such marriages, regardless of where the couple currently resides. Windsor and the DOL's guidance established a conflict between state law (many of which prohibited same-sex marriage) and federal law, which provided that same-sex benefits had to be treated equally under ERISA.

In Obergefell v. Hodges, 135 S.Ct. 2584 (2015), The Supreme Court held, five-to-four, with Justice Kennedy writing for the majority, the right to marry is a fundamental right inherent in the liberty of the person, and under the Due Process and Equal Protection clauses of the Fourteenth Amendment couples of the same sex may not be deprived of that right and liberty. Also, states must recognize same-sex marriages performed in other states.

In a sense, the *Obergefell* case simplifies health benefits because there is only one rule that applies to all employees in all states. Nevertheless, there is still a level of uncertainty or confusion. Although the Affordable Care Act requires employers to offer coverage to employees (or they will be assessed a penalty), employers are not required to offer health plan coverage to spouses. Also, a spouse who is covered by an employee's health insurance is entitled to 36 months of health care continuation (at no more than 102% of cost) in the event of the participant's termination of employment, or the couple's divorce or legal separation. See pp. 537–538 in the main volume.

CHAPTER 7

EMPLOYEE LIBERTY

A. APPEARANCE

1. GROOMING

Page 607. Please add the following note.

5A. In EEOC v. Catastrophe Management Solutions, 852 F.3d 1018 (11th Cir. 2016), Chastity Jones was hired as a customer service representative, a position that did not have contact with the public. Her offer was rescinded, however, when she refused to cut her dreadlocks. The employer's grooming policy called for hairstyle to reflect a "business/professional image." The EEOC alleged that the employer's policy constituted race discrimination because "dreadlocks are a manner of wearing hair that is physiologically and culturally associated with people of African descent." The Eleventh Circuit affirmed dismissal of the case on the ground that race discrimination does not entail cultural practices.

2. DRESS

Page 613. Please delete the principal case and replace with the following.

EEOC v. Abercrombie & Fitch Stores, Inc.

135 S.Ct. 2028 (2015).

■ JUSTICE SCALIA delivered the opinion of the Court.

Title VII of the Civil Rights Act of 1964 prohibits a prospective employer from refusing to hire an applicant in order to avoid accommodating a religious practice that it could accommodate without undue hardship. The question presented is whether this prohibition applies only where an applicant has informed the employer of his need for an accommodation.

I

We summarize the facts in the light most favorable to the Equal Employment Opportunity Commission (EEOC), against whom the Tenth Circuit granted summary judgment. Respondent Abercrombie & Fitch Stores, Inc., operates several lines of clothing stores, each with its own "style." Consistent with the image Abercrombie seeks to project for each store, the company imposes a Look Policy that governs its employees' dress. The Look Policy prohibits "caps"—a term the Policy does not define—as too informal for Abercrombie's desired image.

Samantha Elauf is a practicing Muslim who, consistent with her understanding of her religion's requirements, wears a headscarf. She applied for a position in an Abercrombie store, and was interviewed by Heather Cooke, the store's assistant manager. Using Abercrombie's ordinary system for evaluating applicants, Cooke gave Elauf a rating that qualified her to be hired; Cooke was concerned, however, that Elauf's headscarf would conflict with the store's Look Policy.

Cooke sought the store manager's guidance to clarify whether the headscarf was a forbidden "cap." When this yielded no answer, Cooke turned to Randall Johnson, the district manager. Cooke informed Johnson that she believed Elauf wore her headscarf because of her faith. Johnson told Cooke that Elauf's headscarf would violate the Look Policy, as would all other headwear, religious or otherwise, and directed Cooke not to hire Elauf.

The EEOC sued Abercrombie on Elauf's behalf, claiming that its refusal to hire Elauf violated Title VII. The District Court granted the EEOC summary judgment on the issue of liability, 798 F.Supp.2d 1272 (N.D.Okla.2011), held a trial on damages, and awarded $20,000. The Tenth Circuit reversed and awarded Abercrombie summary judgment. 731 F.3d 1106 (2013). It concluded that ordinarily an employer cannot be liable under Title VII for failing to accommodate a religious practice until the applicant (or employee) provides the employer with actual knowledge of his need for an accommodation. We granted certiorari.

II

Title VII of the Civil Rights Act of 1964, as amended, prohibits two categories of employment practices. It is unlawful for an employer:

"(1) to fail or refuse to hire or to discharge any individual, or otherwise to discriminate against any individual with respect to his compensation, terms, conditions, or privileges of employment, because of such individual's race, color, religion, sex, or national origin; or

(2) to limit, segregate, or classify his employees or applicants for employment in any way which would deprive or tend to deprive any individual of employment opportunities or otherwise adversely affect his status as an employee, because of such individual's race, color, religion, sex, or national origin."

These two proscriptions, often referred to as the "disparate treatment" (or "intentional discrimination") provision and the "disparate impact" provision, are the only causes of action under Title VII. The word "religion" is defined to "includ[e] all aspects of religious observance and practice, as well as belief, unless an employer demonstrates that he is unable to reasonably accommodate to" a "religious observance or practice without undue hardship on the conduct of the employer's business."

Abercrombie's primary argument is that an applicant cannot show disparate treatment without first showing that an employer has "actual knowledge" of the applicant's need for an accommodation. We disagree. Instead, an applicant need only show that his need for an accommodation was a motivating factor in the employer's decision.

The disparate-treatment provision forbids employers to: (1) "fail . . . to hire" an applicant (2) "because of" (3) "such individual's . . . religion" (which includes his religious practice). Here, of course, Abercrombie (1) failed to hire Elauf. The parties concede that (if Elauf sincerely believes that her religion so requires) Elauf's wearing of a headscarf is (3) a "religious practice." All that remains is whether she was not hired (2) "because of" her religious practice.

The term "because of" appears frequently in antidiscrimination laws. It typically imports, at a minimum, the traditional standard of but-for causation. Title VII relaxes this standard, however, to prohibit even making a protected characteristic a "motivating factor" in an employment decision. "Because of" in § 2000e–2(a)(1) links the forbidden consideration to each of the verbs preceding it; an individual's actual religious practice may not be a motivating factor in failing to hire, in refusing to hire, and so on.

It is significant that § 2000e–2(a)(1) does not impose a knowledge requirement. As Abercrombie acknowledges, some antidiscrimination statutes do. For example, the Americans with Disabilities Act of 1990 defines discrimination to include an employer's failure to make "reasonable accommodations to the known physical or mental limitations" of an applicant. Title VII contains no such limitation.

Instead, the intentional discrimination provision prohibits certain motives, regardless of the state of the actor's knowledge. Motive and knowledge are separate concepts. An employer who has actual knowledge of the need for an accommodation does not violate Title VII by refusing to hire an applicant if avoiding that accommodation is not his motive. Conversely, an employer who acts with the motive of avoiding accommodation may violate Title VII even if he has no more than an unsubstantiated suspicion that accommodation would be needed.

Thus, the rule for disparate-treatment claims based on a failure to accommodate a religious practice is straightforward: An employer may not make an applicant's religious practice, confirmed or otherwise, a factor in employment decisions. For example, suppose that an employer thinks (though he does not know for certain) that a job applicant may be an orthodox Jew who will observe the Sabbath, and thus be unable to work on Saturdays. If the applicant actually requires an accommodation of that religious practice, and the employer's desire to avoid the prospective accommodation is a motivating factor in his decision, the employer violates Title VII.

Abercrombie urges this Court to adopt the Tenth Circuit's rule "allocat[ing] the burden of raising a religious conflict." This would require the employer to have actual knowledge of a conflict between an applicant's religious practice and a work rule. The problem with this approach is the one that inheres in most incorrect interpretations of statutes: It asks us to add words to the law to produce what is thought to be a desirable result. That is Congress's province. We construe Title VII's silence as exactly that: silence. Its disparate-treatment provision prohibits actions taken with the motive of avoiding the need for accommodating a religious practice. A request for accommodation, or the employer's certainty that the practice exists, may make it easier to infer motive, but is not a necessary condition of liability.

Abercrombie argues in the alternative that a claim based on a failure to accommodate an applicant's religious practice must be raised as a disparate-impact claim, not a disparate-treatment claim. We think not. That might have been true if Congress had limited the meaning of "religion" in Title VII to religious belief—so that discriminating against a particular religious practice would not be disparate treatment though it might have disparate impact. In fact, however, Congress defined "religion," for Title VII's purposes, as "includ[ing] all aspects of religious observance and practice, as well as belief." Thus, religious practice is one of the protected characteristics that cannot be accorded disparate treatment and must be accommodated.

Nor does the statute limit disparate-treatment claims to only those employer policies that treat religious practices less favorably than similar secular practices. Abercrombie's argument that a neutral policy cannot constitute "intentional discrimination" may make sense in other contexts. But Title VII does not demand mere neutrality with regard to religious practices—that they be treated no worse than other practices. Rather, it gives them favored treatment, affirmatively obligating employers not "to fail or refuse to hire or discharge any individual . . . because of such individual's" "religious observance and practice." An employer is surely entitled to have, for example, a no-headwear policy as an ordinary matter. But when an applicant requires an accommodation as an "aspec[t] of religious . . . practice," it is no response that the subsequent "fail[ure] . . . to hire" was due to an otherwise-neutral policy. Title VII requires otherwise-neutral policies to give way to the need for an accommodation.

* * *

The Tenth Circuit misinterpreted Title VII's requirements in granting summary judgment. We reverse its judgment and remand the case for further consideration consistent with this opinion.

It is so ordered.

■ JUSTICE ALITO, concurring in the judgment.

* * *

■ JUSTICE THOMAS, concurring in the judgment.

* * *

I would hold that Abercrombie's conduct did not constitute "intentional discrimination." Abercrombie refused to create an exception to its neutral Look Policy for Samantha Elauf's religious practice of wearing a headscarf. In doing so, it did not treat religious practices less favorably than similar secular practices, but instead remained neutral with regard to religious practices. To be sure, the *effects* of Abercrombie's neutral Look Policy, absent an accommodation, fall more harshly on those who wear headscarves as an aspect of their faith. But that is a classic case of an alleged disparate impact. It is not what we have previously understood to be a case of disparate treatment because Elauf received the *same* treatment from Abercrombie as any other applicant who appeared unable to comply with the company's Look Policy. Because I cannot classify Abercrombie's conduct as "intentional discrimination," I would affirm.

QUESTIONS

1.   Suppose the employer's agent, unaware of the likely religious significance of the headscarf she wore to the interview, refused to hire Elauf because she thought the color of Elauf's headscarf "clashed" with her dress and therefore she believed Elauf lacked the sense of style to be a sales associate for Abercrombie & Fitch. Would this be actionable religious discrimination? How would you apply the reasoning of the majority?

2.   Suppose the employer's agent knew that another applicant was not a Muslim and refused to hire her because he thought it was "wrong" for a non-Muslim to wear an assumedly Muslim headscarf. Would this violate Title VII?

3.   Suppose yet another applicant was not a Muslim and wore a headscarf simply because she liked the way it looked. Further suppose that the employer refused to hire her because it erroneously believed she *was* a Muslim. Would this be a violation of Title VII? Compare the "regarded as" provision of the ADA. Does there need to be a "regarded as" provision for Title VII?

4.   For a further discussion of *Abercrombie,* see Jeffrey M. Hirsch, *EEOC v. Abercrombie & Fitch Stores, Inc.:* Mistakes, Same-Sex Marriage, and Unintended Consequences, 94 Tex. L. Rev. 95 (2016); Michael C. Harper, Confusion on the Court: Distinguishing Disparate Treatment from Disparate Impact in *Young v. UPS* and *EEOC v. Abercrombie & Fitch, Inc.,* 96 B.U.L. Rev. 543 (2016).

5.   A similar issue was raised before the European Union Court of Justice, the highest court of the EU. A Muslim woman in Belgium, Samira Achbita, was fired from her job as a receptionist at a security company because she wore a head scarf. The court held that the employer's "neutral rule" prohibited the wearing of visible signs of political, philosophical, or religious beliefs and therefore it did not treat any employees differently in violation of

EU Council Directive 2000/78/EC. In a companion case, the court stated that "customer preference" is not a defense. See Court of Justice Press Release No. 30/17 (March 14, 2017), available at www.curia.europe.eu.

C. FREEDOM OF EXPRESSION

1. PUBLIC SECTOR

Page 658. Please add the following notes.

3A. A police sergeant with 25 years of service posted on her Facebook page comments highly critical of the police chief because he did not permit officers to use their police cars to attend the funeral of an officer killed in the line of duty in a surrounding town. Are the postings protected under *Garcetti*, thereby allowing her to challenge her subsequent discharge? See Graziosi v. City of Greenville, 775 F.3d 731 (5th Cir. 2015) (held: no; speech was not on a matter of public concern). See also Brown v. Chicago Board of Educ., 824 F.3d 713 (7th Cir. 2016) (statements made in classroom by a teacher are within official duties and therefore not about a public concern); Rock v. Levinski, 791 F.3d 1215 (10th Cir. 2015) (statement by school principal opposing school district's plan to close her school was not protected because it was a statement by a policymaking individual with the potential to have a detrimental impact on close working relationships).

6A. In Liverman v. City of Petersburg, 844 F.3d 400 (4th Cir. 2016), the Fourth Circuit held that the police department's social media policy, prohibiting all posts that tended to discredit or reflect unfavorably on the department, was overbroad. "The advent of social media does not provide cover for the airing of purely personal grievances, but neither can it provide a pretext for shutting off meaningful discussion of larger public issues in this new public sphere." Id. at 414.

2. PRIVATE SECTOR

Page 664. Please add the following note.

5. Private sector employees may be extended free speech rights in the workplace by state statute. See, e.g., Trusz v. UBS Realty Investors, LLC, 123 A.3d 1212 (Conn. 2015).

E. COLLECTIVE ACTION

Page 674. Please add the following note.

2A. Although employees have a right to engage in protected concerted activity, it is sometimes a close case as to whether the conduct of the employees cross the line into misconduct, thereby justifying discipline or termination by the employer. In DIRECTV, Inc. v. NLRB, 837 F.3d 25 (D.C. Cir. 2016), employees unhappy with a new pay policy aired their grievances ibn an interview with a reported for a local television news station. The D.C. Circuit held that the "third party appeal" in the interview was protected and, quoting the NLRB, said it was not "flagrantly disloyal, wholly incommensurate with any grievances which they might have."

Page 674. Please delete Note 6 and replace with the following.

6. In NLRB v. J. Weingarten, Inc., 420 U.S. 251 (1975), the Supreme Court held that an employee has a right to have a union representative present at an investigatory interview. The NLRB has changed its view on whether these so-called *Weingarten* rights also extend to nonunion employees. In its latest decision, IBM Corp., 341 NLRB 148 (2004), the NLRB (3–2) held that the right to have a coworker present at an investigatory interview does not extend to nonunion employees. The Board relied on the need for prompt investigatory interviews because of the threat of terrorism. "Further, because of the events of Sept. 11, 2001 and the aftermath, we must now take into account the presence of both real and threatened attacks. We hold that the *Weingarten* right does not extend to the non-union workplace." Should the possibility of exigent circumstances justify the rule or the exception?

F. REGULATION OF OFF-WORK ACTIVITY

2. POLITICAL ACTIVITY

Page 688. Please add the following note.

2A. Heffernan v. City of Paterson, 136 S.Ct. 1412 (2016), involved a police officer working in the office of the chief of police of Paterson, New Jersey. Both the chief of police and Heffernan's supervisor had been appointed by the mayor, who was running for re-election against Spagnola, a good friend of Heffernan's. Heffernan was not involved in Sapgnola's campaign in any capacity. As a favor to his bedridden mother, Heffernan agreed to pick up a Spagnola campaign yard sign to replace one that had been stolen. When Heffernan was observed by other police officers while holding a Spagnola yard sign, word spread throughout the force and Heffernan was demoted from a detective to a patrol officer because of his "overt involvement" in Spagnola's campaign. Heffernan brought suit under section 1983, arguing that he had been demoted in violation of his First Amendment rights. The district court and the Third Circuit held that Heffernan's case was actionable only if his employer's conduct was prompted by his actual, rather than his perceived, exercise of free-speech rights. The Supreme Court, 6–2, reversed in an opinion by Justice Breyer. "When an employer demotes an employee out of a desire to prevent the employee from engaging in political activity that the First Amendment protects, the employee is entitled to challenge that unlawful action under the First Amendment and 42 U.S.C. § 1983— even if, as here, the employer makes a factual mistake about the employee's behavior." 136 S.Ct. at 1418. In dissent, Justice Thomas (with Justice Alito) argued, as had the Third Circuit, that Heffernan had no cause of action because his constitutional rights had not been violated.

3. LIFESTYLE

Page 696. Please add the following note.

4A. Two sheriff's deputies moved in with each other's wives (i.e., swapped wives) before getting divorced from their current wives. They were discharged for violating the Sherriff's Code of Conduct, which banned "any illegal, immoral, or indecent conduct." They had also violated a provision requiring them to inform their supervisors within 24 hours of a change of address. Is their discharge unconstitutional? See Coker v. Whittington, 858 F.3d 304 (5th Cir.), cert. denied, 138 S.Ct. 559 (2017) (held: no). But cf. Perez v. City of Roseville, 882 F.3d 843 (9th Cir. 2018) (holding that a probationary police officer's constitutional rights to privacy and intimate association were violated if it can be established that the discharge was because of a romantic relationship with a fellow officer).

CHAPTER 8

OCCUPATIONAL SAFETY AND HEALTH

A. INTRODUCTION

1. BACKGROUND

Page 705. Please add the following note.

1A. Section 701 of the Bipartisan Budget Act of 2015 (Pub. L. No. 114–74) contains a provision requiring OSHA to increase the maximum penalties through a one-time "catch-up" increase based on the Consumer Price Index (CPI) since 1990. From 1990 to 2015 the CPI increased 82%. OSHA is also required to increase maximum penalties by the amount of inflation in the prior year. As of January 2, 2018, the maximum OSHA penalties are as follows:

De minimis notice	$0
Nonserious	$0–$12,934
Serious	$1–$12,934
Repeated	$0–$129,336
Willful	$9,239–$129,336

2. JURISDICTION

Page 717. Please add the following to Note 9.

In Lucas v. Beckman Coulter, Inc., 811 S.E.2d 369 (Ga. 2018), an employee took his handgun with him in a company-owned car on a service call to a customer's premises when he accidentally shot the plaintiff. In an action against the employee and the employer, the employer argued that it was immune from liability by virtue of a state statute granting immunity to employers for harms resulting from firearms being stored in an employee's automobile, such as those resulting from a theft of firearms from the automobile. The Supreme Court of Georgia held that the statute did not immunize employers from all firearm-related tort actions, including injuries resulting from an employee taking a firearm in a company-owned vehicle off the employer's property.

With regard to governmental immunity, compare Lane v. City & Borough of Juneau, 2018 WL 1977730 (Alaska 2018) (city not immune from liability for handgun-related injuries caused by city employee within scope of employment) with Kohler v. HP Enterprise Services, LLC, 212 F.Supp.3d 1 (D.D.C. 2016) (government contractor immune from liability where employee acted outside his scope of employment and opened fire at Navy shipyard).

B. PROMULGATION OF STANDARDS

2. NEW STANDARDS

Page 728. Please add the following note.

5. For an article proposing a new, more expansive approach to "feasibility" under section 6(b)(5), see Jason R. Bent, Health Theft, 48 U. Conn. L. Rev. 637 (2016).

C. EMPLOYER DUTIES

2. GENERAL DUTY CLAUSE

Page 740. Please add the following to the end of Note 3.

In Western World, Inc. v. Secretary of Labor, 604 F. Appx. 188 (3d Cir. 2015), cert. denied 136 S.Ct. 1161 (2016), the court affirmed a section 5(a)(1) violation arising at the employer's Wild West theme park where an actor staging a gun fight mistakenly used live bullets and shot another actor in the head. The OSHA violation was the employer's failure to prohibit employees from using their own firearms, which were capable of shooting live bullets.

F. NON-OSHA SAFETY AND HEALTH LAW

Page 768. Please add the following to Note 4.

On an employer's duty to accommodate a pregnant employee under the PDA, see Young v. UPS, p. 52 in this supplement.

CHAPTER 9

DISABLING INJURY AND ILLNESS

B. WORKERS' COMPENSATION COVERAGE

1. "EMPLOYEE"

Page 778. Please add the following to Note 3.

Some workers' compensation claimants have successfully challenged exclusions from coverage under state law. See, e.g., S.G. Borello & Sons, Inc. v. Department of Industrial Relations, 769 P.2d 399 (Cal. 1989) (agricultural workers are not independent contractors and therefore are eligible for workers' compensation); Rodriguez v. Brand West Dairy, 378 P.3d 13 (N.M. 2016) (violation of equal protection under New Mexico Constitution to exclude farm and ranch laborers from coverage).

2. "COURSE OF EMPLOYMENT"

Pages 782–784. Please insert the following notes.

2A. In Layne v. Crist Elec. Contractor, Inc., 768 S.E.2d 261 (Va. App. 2015), an employee suffered severe injuries when a scissor lift he was operating was struck by a crane, and he plunged to the floor in a large warehouse. The Virginia Court of Appeals held that the claimant was not entitled to workers' compensation benefits because his violation of the "lock-out-tagout" safety rule was a willful violation. The employee knew of the rule and had followed it in the past. He was unable to explain his failure in the case because his severe brain injuries prevented him from testifying. What does it mean to "willfully" violate a safety standard?

2B. Bates and McDaniel were employees at a sugar cooperative. While performing his work duties Bates encountered McDaniel and began attacking him with a brass hammer because Bates had discovered on the Internet that McDaniel is a registered sex offender. Bates was immediately fired, and McDaniel filed for workers' compensation benefits. Is McDaniel entitled to recover for the injuries caused by his coworker? See McDaniel v. Western Sugar Coop., 867 N.W.2d 302 (Neb. Ct. App. 2015) (held: no; the injury did not "arise out of" employment because it was not caused by or exacerbated by the employment).

3A. The business manager of a Girl Scout summer camp went on an end-of-the-season horseback ride with other staff members. Her horse unexpectedly bolted, throwing her in the air and seriously injuring her back. Is she entitled to workers' compensation? See Pollock v. Girl Scouts of Southern Ala., Inc., 176 So. 3d 222 (Ala. Ct. App. 2015) (held: no; injury occurred during voluntary recreational activity).

3B. In Calumet School District #132 v. Illinois Workers' Comp. Comm'n, 67 N.E.3d 966 (Ill. Ct. App. 2016), a teacher was injured in an after-school basketball game with students. The teacher only agreed to participate because he was pressured to do so by the principal. In upholding an award of benefits, the court held that the basketball game was not a "voluntary recreational program" under the Illinois statute, which would have made his injury noncompensable.

6A. A firefighter and emergency technician was working a required 24-hour shift and was sleeping in accommodations supplied by his employer for this purpose. During the night, he dreamed that spiders were crawling on him, and to avoid them he jumped out of bed, injuring his foot. In his workers' compensation claim, he argued that his injury was caused by his employer-provided sleeping arrangements. The employer argued that his injury was "idiopathic," peculiar to the individual and unrelated to employment. Is the employee entitled to compensation? See Hansen v. City of Siloam Springs, 541 S.W.3d 473 (Ark. Ct. App. 2018) (held: no). What if the employee fell from an upper bunk bed, with or without dreaming about spiders?

C. OCCUPATIONAL DISEASE

2. BURDEN OF PROOF

Page 792. Please insert the following case before section D.

Kilburn v. Granite State Insurance Co.

522 S.W.3d 384 (Tenn. 2017).

■ ROGER A. PAGE, J.:

* * *

I.   Facts and Procedural History

On November 6, 2008, Charles Kilburn, a trim carpenter, was severely injured in a motor vehicle accident during the course of his employment. His employer was Ryan Brown ("Employer"). As a result of the accident, Mr. Kilburn incurred fractures to the C3 and C4 vertebrae in his neck and disc herniations at the L4-5 and L5-S1 areas of his lower back. Dr. Jacob Schwarz, a neurosurgeon, performed an anterior cervical discectomy and surgical fusion of the C3 and C4 vertebrae on July 29, 2009, which improved Mr. Kilburn's neck pain. After physical therapy and an epidural steroid injection, Mr. Kilburn still complained of severe back pain when bending forward or backward, pain that was more severe on his left side than on the right, and lower extremity pain. Mr. Kilburn also felt heaviness in his legs after walking for a short period of time such that he would have to sit down, which Dr. Schwarz opined was a symptom of neurogenic claudication. As a result, Dr. Schwarz recommended surgery to the L4-5 and L5-S1 areas of Mr. Kilburn's lower back. However, Mr. Kilburn's insurance company denied coverage for the surgery due to a peer review by three physicians disagreeing with Dr.

Schwarz's findings. The insurance company also denied Dr. Schwarz's recommendation for epidural steroid injections. Dr. Schwarz then referred Mr. Kilburn to a pain management clinic and wrote a letter to Mr. Kilburn's insurance adjustor asserting that Mr. Kilburn's pain was debilitating enough to prevent him from returning to work.

On January 4, 2010, Mr. Kilburn was evaluated by Dr. William Leone, a pain management specialist. Dr. Leone's notes reflect that he was concerned with Mr. Kilburn's consumption of alcohol while taking his medication. Mr. Kilburn also admitted that because he felt the medication was no longer effective, he was taking two opioid tablets at once even though he had only been prescribed one tablet at a time. The urinary drug screen conducted that day showed the presence of both alcohol and the opioid medication. As a result, Dr. Leone recommended weaning Mr. Kilburn off the opioid medication and trying other options. Dr. Leone prescribed 350 mg of Soma twice daily and 15 mg of oxycodone four times daily. As part of his treatment, Mr. Kilburn initialed and signed an agreement stating, "I will control my usage of narcotic medications as directed by the attending physician. There are no exceptions. If medication is inadequate for [my] pain level, [I] must call before adjusting dosage."

During the trial, Phillip Manning, Mr. Kilburn's brother-in-law, and Judy Kilburn, Mr. Kilburn's wife, explained that prior to the 2008 motor vehicle accident, Mr. Kilburn was friendly and outgoing and was very active. However, after the injury and neck surgery, Mr. Kilburn's lower back pain seemed to Mr. Manning to be "[p]retty bad" and uncomfortable, and Mr. Kilburn was "upset" about not being able to have the lower back surgery. Mr. Manning opined that Mr. Kilburn "had anxiety about not having medication and not having the surgery" but that Mr. Kilburn never appeared hopeless, just ready to be back to full capacity. Mr. Manning stated that Mr. Kilburn started skipping doses of his medication because he was scared that he was going to run out of the medication and would be unable to obtain more.

* * *

Ms. Kilburn found Mr. Kilburn unresponsive in bed on the morning of January 28, 2010. The medical examiner's report specifically stated that the cause of death was acute oxycodone toxicity with contributory causes of hypertension, tobacco use, and alcohol use. His death was deemed an accident. Mr. Kilburn was forty years old at the time of his death.

At trial, Dr. Alistair Finlayson and Dr. Jeffrey Hazlewood testified by deposition about their review of Mr. Kilburn's medical records. Dr. Finlayson was a psychiatrist with a subspecialty in addictions and a clinical associate professor in psychiatry at Vanderbilt University Medical Center. He was also the medical director of the Comprehensive Assessment Program at Vanderbilt, which evaluates professionals to determine if they are "fit for duty." He performed a records review at the request of Ms. Kilburn. Dr. Finlayson stated that it was "more likely than not" that Mr. Kilburn was suffering from severe pain or anxiety at the time of his death and that it was "certainly possible" that those conditions diminished Mr. Kilburn's faculties and contributed to his risk of overdose.

* * *

Dr. Finlayson stated that when a person is used to taking an opioid but then takes less or stops taking the medication, "the pain is intensified and anxiety is intensified as a . . . withdrawal." Dr. Finlayson stated that drugs like OxyContin, Soma, and Valium all contribute to feelings of depression and hopelessness, which could potentially influence a person's judgment. He further opined that he did not believe that Mr. Kilburn was addicted to his medication but rather that "it [was] possible that . . . he was so discouraged, depressed, anxious about what was going to happen and experiencing some withdrawal symptoms that he . . . took maybe more medication than he intended to, combined with more alcohol than he intended to."

* * *

Dr. Hazlewood was a board-certified physician in physical medicine, rehabilitation, and pain management and had been practicing in pain management for nineteen years. He conducted a records review at the request of the Employer. Dr. Hazlewood agreed with Dr. Leone's recommendation to slowly decrease Mr. Kilburn's intake of narcotics, rather than increasing the dosage, because of Mr. Kilburn's building tolerance to the medication and because of Mr. Kilburn's use of alcohol. He opined that taking 60 mg of oxycodone daily along with consuming alcohol was inadvisable. When discussing the effect of Mr. Kilburn's pain and anxiety on his judgment, Dr. Hazlewood stated that while acute pain such as breaking several bones at one time can cloud a person's judgment, he did not think that chronic pain such as Mr. Kilburn's could cloud a person's judgment. Dr. Hazlewood agreed that anxiety, depression, and suicidal ideations could cloud a person's judgment but stated that he was not qualified to state whether pain can cause an anxiety disorder.

* * *

Both doctors agreed that while tobacco use and hypertension were tangentially related to Mr. Kilburn's health and ability to withstand the acute oxycodone toxicity, Mr. Kilburn's use of alcohol was the primary contributing factor.

After hearing the evidence, the trial court issued its decision as a written memorandum. The trial court accredited the opinion of Dr. Finlayson over that of Dr. Hazlewood. The court found that Ms. Kilburn had sustained her burden of proof to show that Mr. Kilburn's death was a direct and natural consequence of his work injury. It awarded workers' compensation death benefits to Ms. Kilburn. Employer has timely appealed, asserting that the evidence preponderates against the trial court's finding of compensability and that Mr. Kilburn's conduct constituted an independent intervening cause of his death.

* * *

III. Analysis

* * *

"The basic rule is that a subsequent injury, whether an aggravation of the original injury or a new and distinct injury, is compensable if it is the direct and natural result of a compensable primary injury." Therefore, " 'all the medical consequences and sequelae that flow from the primary injury are compensable.' " Anderson v. Westfield Grp., 259 S.W.3d 690, 696 (Tenn. 2008) (quoting 1 Larson's Workers' Compensation Law § 10.01 (2004)). However, that rule has a limit that "hinges on whether the subsequent injury is the result of independent intervening causes, such as the employee's own conduct." Stated another way, " 'the progressive worsening or complication of a work-connected injury remains compensable so long as the worsening is not shown to have been produced by an intervening nonindustrial cause.' " The *Anderson* court provided several examples of cases in which the injured employee's conduct constituted an independent intervening cause that rendered the subsequent injury to be non-compensable: Simpson v. H.D. Lee Co., 793 S.W.2d 929, 931–32 (Tenn. 1990) (concluding that medication taken contrary to instructions constituted an intervening cause); Guill v. Aetna Life & Cas. Co., 660 S.W.2d 42, 43–44 (Tenn. 1983) (determining that injecting medication contrary to medical instructions was an intervening cause); and Jones v. Huey, 210 Tenn. 162, 357 S.W.2d 47, 49–50 (1962) (deciding that the negligent operation of a tractor after a work-related back injury was not compensable). The *Anderson* Court adopted the reasoning of Jones v. Huey and stated:

> [W]e reject the employee's argument that only reckless or intentional misconduct can constitute an intervening cause. Instead, we find, as we did in *Jones*, that negligence is the appropriate standard for determining whether an independent intervening cause relieves an employer of liability for a subsequent injury purportedly flowing from a prior work-related injury.

Anderson, 259 S.W.3d at 698–99. Application of the intervening cause principle is not an affirmative defense but, rather, is a "way of assessing the scope of an employer's liability for injuries occurring after a compensable injury."

* * *

Based on the above analysis, we conclude that the evidence preponderates against the trial court's findings. We conclude that * * * Mr. Kilburn failed to take his pain medication in accordance with his physician's instructions, which ultimately caused his demise. Therefore, his death was no longer causally related to his work-related injury, and his overdose was an independent intervening cause.

Conclusion

In summary, we conclude that Mr. Kilburn's failure to consume his medication in accordance with his doctor's instructions was an independent intervening cause. As such, we reverse the judgment of the trial court. The costs of this appeal are taxed to the plaintiff, Judy Kilburn.

QUESTIONS

1.   Most courts hold that claimants are entitled to additional compensation for the aggravation of an injury or illness attributable to medical malpractice. Should the additional harm caused by the "negligence" of the claimant be compensable?

2.   Accidents caused by employee negligence are compensable under the no-fault scheme of workers' compensation. Should employee fault in the aggravation of an injury be compensable? A woman slipped and fell while walking to work, incurring multiple injuries for which she received compensation. Years later, she requested and was denied additional benefits to treat her lumbar spondylosis, a new condition she argued was a "flow-through" from her original injuries. Expert testimony, however, found that her failure to lose weight, combined with natural aging was the proximate cause of her current ailment, not her prior slip and fall. Accordingly, the court affirmed the denial of additional compensation. Leasure v. UVMC, 2017 WL 3446986 (Ohio Ct. App. 2017).

3.   In light of the crisis of opioid misuse, would it violate public policy to award compensation for opioid misuse? In an unpublished opinion, the North Carolina Court of Appeals affirmed that an employee's accidental overdose of opioids, among other drugs prescribed to treat a work injury, was compensable. The court held that the original work injury was a proximate cause of the overdose death. Brady v. Best Buy Co., 2017 N.C. App. LEXIS 844 (2017). By contrast, an Arkansas court held that an intentional opioid overdose constituted an independent and intervening cause of death (an employee overdosed on methadone while in recovery from addiction to the opioids that were prescribed to treat a compensable injury) and denied workers' compensation death benefits. Loar v. Cooper Tire & Rubber Co., No. CV-13-1128, 2014 Ark. App. 240 (Ark. Ct. App. 2014).

D. DETERMINING BENEFIT LEVELS

2. REHABILITATION AND OTHER SERVICES

Page 806. Please add the following to Note 4.

See Turner v. Southern Alloy & Metals Corp., 521 S.W.3d 515 (Ark. Ct. App. 2017) (claimant, permanently and totally disabled due to work-related injury in 1975, was not entitled to a new van to accommodate his electric wheelchair based on state statute that was amended in 1993).

PART IV

TERMINATING THE RELATIONSHIP

CHAPTER 10

DISCHARGE

A. STATUTORY AND CONSTITUTIONAL PROTECTIONS OF EMPLOYEES

1. WHISTLEBLOWER LAWS

Page 850. Please insert as new notes.

6. The Homeland Security Act, enacted in 2002, requires the Transportation Security Administration to prohibit disclosure of information detrimental to transportation security. MacLean, a federal air marshal, believed that cancelling certain missions from Las Vegas was dangerous and illegal. He told a newspaper reporter about the TSA decision he didn't like. TSA fired him. MacLean sued, alleging that his disclosure was whistleblowing protected by a federal statute protecting employees who disclose "any violation of any law, rule, or regulation," or "a substantial . . . danger to public . . . safety." The Supreme Court ruled for MacLean, saying that the exception to whistleblowing protection for leaking information in violation of law did not create an exception for violations of the regulation TSA had issued concerning "sensitive security information." A regulation, said the Court majority, is not a "law." Dep't of Homeland Sec. v. MacLean, 135 S.Ct. 913 (2015) (7–2).

7. Menendez complained to Halliburton management about what he thought were questionable accounting practices. He also complained to the SEC. Halliburton let Menendez's colleagues know that he had been the whistleblower. The colleagues, whom he had essentially accused of fraud, ostracized him. Held: What Halliburton did was illegal retaliation under section 806 of the Sarbanes-Oxley Act. Halliburton, Inc. v. Admin. Rev. Bd., 771 F.3d 254 (5th Cir. 2014).

8. Henry Roop was fired by Southern Pharmaceuticals Corporation (SPC) one day after he told his boss on the telephone that another executive had offered to make payments to the wife of Patrick Gregory, clinical coordinator at Central Medical Health Services, if Gregory referred diabetic equipment purchases to SPC. The wife, Josephine, would not be expected to perform work for SPC. The Mississippi Supreme Court said the jury had enough evidence to conclude that Roop was fired for reporting conduct that violated the federal Medicare and Medicaid Anti-Kickback statute and that terminating him for that reason violated the "narrow public-policy exception to Mississippi's employment-at-will doctrine." Roop v. Southern Pharm. Corp., 188 So.3d 1179 (Miss. 2016).

9. One of the most common statutes whistleblowers seek protection under is the False Claims Act (FCA). 31 U.S.C. §§ 3729, 3730(b–g). The FCA empowers private plaintiffs to bring suits on behalf of the government against persons who knowingly present false or fraudulent claims to the government for approval or payment. In Universal Health Services Inc. v. US ex rel Julio Escobar, 136 S.Ct. 1989 (2016), the Supreme Court expanded the basis upon which these claims can be made. Specifically, the Court held that false claims may be the basis for liability when two conditions are satisfied: (1) the claim does not merely request payment, but also makes specific representations about the goods or services provided; and (2) the defendant's failure to disclose noncompliance with material statutory, regulatory, or contractual requirements makes those representations misleading half-truths.

10. Dodd-Frank only protects an employee who reports securities-law violations to the SEC. There is no protection for an employee who reports a violation to management and then asserts that his or her dismissal was unlawful retaliation. Digital Realty Trust, Inc. v. Somers, 138 S.Ct. 767 (2018).

2. CONSTITUTIONAL PROTECTIONS

Page 859. Please add the following notes.

10. Linhoff had worked at University of Connecticut Health Center for 15 years as a "skilled maintainer . . . changing heating, ventilation and air conditioning filters on hospital roof" with no prior discipline. A police officer spotted him sitting with a coworker in a state van while smoking marijuana. He was fired. The arbitrator under a public employee union contract said Linhoff should be suspended from work for 6 months without pay and after that experience random drug testing for a year. Connecticut appealed and the trial court said Linhoff should be terminated. The Supreme Court reversed and approved the arbitrator's much lighter punishment, saying it did not violate public policy. State of Connecticut v. Connecticut Employees Union, 142 A.3d 1122 (Conn. 2016).

But see City of Richfield v. Law Enforcement Labor Services, Inc., 910 N.W.2d 465 (Minn. Ct. of Appeals 2018). A police officer was terminated for failing to report his use of force in violation of the employer's policy. He had previously been disciplined, trained, and counseled for prior infractions. An arbitrator ruled that the officer should be reinstated. The appellate court overturned that decision based on the "clear public policy in favor of transparency . . . on the use of force."

11. When Indiana by state statute revoked tenure rights of public school teachers, it violated the Contracts Clause of the U.S. Constitution. Elliott v. Board of School Trustees, 876 F.3d 926 (7th Cir. 2017), cert. denied, 2018 WL 1243305.

12. Two sheriff's deputies moved in with each other's wives (i.e., traded wives) before getting divorced from their current wives. They were fired for violating the Sheriff's Code of Conduct, which banned "any illegal, immoral, or indecent conduct." They had also violated a provision requiring them to inform their supervisors within 24 hours of a change of address. Held, firing them for this behavior did not violate their constitutional rights. Coker v. Whittington, 858 F.3d 304 (5th Cir. 2017), cert. denied, 138 S.Ct. 559 (2017).

But see Perez v. City of Roseville, 882 F.3d 843 (9th Cir. 2018), holding that a probationary police officer's constitutional privacy and intimate association rights were violated if it can be established that she was discharged because of her romantic relationship with a fellow officer.

3. STATUTORY CONTRACTS—THE MONTANA EXCEPTION

Page 865. Please add the following note.

3. How much evidence does a plaintiff need in order to prove a firing decision was not made for "good cause"? In Moe v. Butte-Silver Bow County, 371 P.3d 415 (Mont. 2016), the plaintiff, a human resources director, was fired for inappropriate conduct and job performance deficiencies articulated in a complaint by a subordinate. The court reversed the district court, finding that there was a genuine issue of material fact as to whether the plaintiff was fired for good cause because the plaintiff's response letter "presented exhaustive responses to the allegations against her." In Bird v. Cascade County, 386 P.3d. 602 (Mont. 2016), the plaintiff, also a human resources director, was terminated for, among other allegations, using public resources for political purposes and disclosing confidential information. Distinguishing *Moe,* the court upheld the decision for summary judgment largely because the majority of the plaintiff's response letter amounted to "conclusory statements, speculative assertions, and mere denials."

C. TORT EXCEPTIONS TO EMPLOYMENT AT WILL

2. PUBLIC POLICY

a. LEGAL DUTIES

Page 921. Please insert after Note 1.

1A. Minnesota's workers' compensation antiretaliation statute is not preempted by federal immigration law from providing legal protection against discharge to an undocumented worker. Anibal Sanchez, who was born in Mexico, had worked for Dahlke as a body shop assistant for about eight years, having obtained the job with a false social security number. Sanchez was injured at work. When he told Doug Smithers, a part-owner and manager, that he had a lawyer who was filing a workers' compensation claim, Smithers replied that he hated lawyers and said, "[T]he bridge between us [is] broken." The majority opinion said that this was unlawful retaliation for seeking workers' compensation benefits, even though it would be unlawful under IRCA (the federal statute) to have him as an employee. The dissent said that Sanchez had not been fired because the company had said that he could return to work if he became legally eligible (i.e. if he solved his immigration status). Sanchez v. Dahlke Trailer Sales, 897 N.W.2d 267 (Minnesota 2017) (6–3).

See also Mera-Hernandez v. U.S.D. 233, 390 P.3d 875 (Kan. 2017). Plaintiff made false statements about her immigration status when she was hired in 2009. Three years later she injured her back and obtained workers' compensation benefits. When her employer discovered her false statements, it fired her. But the Kansas Supreme Court said she should nonetheless receive workers' compensation benefits.

Please add to Note 3.

Does the analysis change if the wrongdoing was used as "pretext" for an otherwise discriminatory termination? Katie Mayes supervised employees on the night-shift freight crew at WinCo, an Idaho Falls grocery store. Because the job was difficult and often required employees to work beyond their shift, Mayes would often take stale cakes from the store's bakery and offer them to her employees in the break room. While Mayes had discussed this practice with management, in 2011 she was fired for her cake "theft." A panel of the Ninth Circuit reversed the district court's summary judgment in favor of the defendant on gender discrimination claims under Title VII, finding that the plaintiff put forth sufficient evidence that WinCo's proffered reasons for the termination were pretexual. See Mayes v. WinCo Holdings Inc. 846 F.3d 1274 (9th Cir. 2017).

Please add note.

5.   Latyoa Ballard worked for Ranchor Manor Healthcare as a nurse. She had a romantic relationship and two children with Jason Henderson, also a nurse. Henderson assaulted Ballard and injured her and one child. A trial court entered a one-year order of protection. Henderson was promoted to be Ballard's supervisor. Rancho Manor said she could keep her job only if she withdrew the order of protection. She said no and was fired. An appellate court held that her dismissal violated Missouri's public policy of protecting victims of domestic violence. Ballard v. The Honorable Ellen Levy Siwak, 521 S.W.3d 296 (Missouri App. 2017).

b.   STATUTORY AND CONSTITUTIONAL RIGHTS

Page 928. Please insert after Note 1.

1A. In a recent post-*Hansen* case, the Utah Supreme Court found that the state treats the right of self-defense as an important public policy. Wal-Mart's policy required employees to disengage and withdraw from potentially violent situations. The company fired several employees who were involved in physical confrontations with shoplifting customers. The court said that their dismissal might violate the public policy tort but limited the exception from at-will employment "to situations where an employee reasonably believes that force is necessary to defend against an imminent threat of serious bodily harm and the employee has no opportunity to withdraw." Ray v. Wal-Mart Stores, Inc., 359 P.3d 614 (Utah 2015). The doctrinal question had been certified to the Utah Supreme Court by the U.S. District Court. See also Swindol v. Aurora Flight Sciences Corp., 832 F.3d 492 (5th Cir. 2016), saying that Mississippi law makes terminating an employee for having a firearm inside his locked vehicle on company property "legally impermissible." This was the first time Mississippi recognized any statutory exception to employment-at-will.

c.   PUBLIC HEALTH AND SAFETY

Page 935. Please add note.

6.   Maddin was a truck driver. Brakes on his trailer froze because of subzero temperatures. After reporting the problem and waiting several hours for a repair truck, Maddin—his torso numb and his feet with no feeling because of the cold—unhitched truck from trailer and drove away. He was terminated for abandoning the trailer. Held, the administrative law judge correctly determined that Maddin was fired in violation of the whistleblower and health and safety provisions of the federal Surface Transportation Assistance Act. Judge Gorsuch (then on 10th Circuit) dissented, saying that the federal law only forbids employers from firing employees who "refuse to operate a vehicle" out of safety concerns and that Maddin therefore should have waited longer in the truck. This is a major Gorsuch anti-*Chevron* opinion, saying courts should apply the words of the statute and not search for Congress's meaning. Transam Trucking, Inc. v. Admin. Rev. Bd., 833 F.3d 1206 (10th Cir. 2016).

d.   STANDARDS OF PROFESSIONAL CONDUCT

Page 936. Add this to the paragraph that runs over from page 935.

A Regional Staff Attorney at an insurance company said he could not handle the workload the company was assigning to him. He was dismissed. He argued that professional norms required him to provide competent representation to his clients and therefore dismissing him violated the Missouri Rules of Professional Conduct. An appellate court ruled against him. "It is a matter of professional opinion and judgment as to when a workload becomes so excessive as to affect an attorney's duty of competence. Thus, [the Rules of Professional Conduct] do not constitute a clear mandate of public policy." DeFoe v. American Family Mutual Insurance Company, 526 S.W.3d 236 (Missouri App. 2017).

CHAPTER 11

EMPLOYEES' DUTIES TO THE EMPLOYER

B. POST-EMPLOYMENT RESTRICTIONS

1. FUTURE EMPLOYMENT

Page 1006. Please insert this note after Note 14.

14A. Socko was a salesperson for a company that provided basement water-proofing services. Three years after starting at the company, he signed a two-year non-compete agreement saying that for two years after leaving that employer, he would not compete in nine specific mid-east states. The agreement said that the parties "intend to be legally bound," but the Pennsylvania Supreme Court said that "when a non-competition clause is required after an employee has commenced his or her employment, it is enforceable only if the employee receives 'new' and valuable consideration—that is, some corresponding benefit or a favorable change in employment status." This can be "a promotion, a change from part-time to full-time employment, or even a change to a compensation package . . ." The mere continuation of employment is insufficient to serve as consideration, "despite it being an at-will relationship terminable by either party." Socko v. Mid-Atlantic Sys. of CPA, Inc., 126 A.3d 1266 (Pa. 2015).

Page 1007. Please add to Note 18.

See Norman Bishara & Evan Starr, The Incomplete Noncompete Picture, 20 Lewis & Clark L. Rev. 497, 508–509 (2016):

> Several states have been experimenting . . . with various models of how to best evaluate or restrict the use of noncompetes for their citizens. For example, Colorado's statute restricts noncompetes to executives making high salaries and their executive assistants. Oregon's non-competition statute . . . requires that an employee asked to sign a non-compete must be provided at least two weeks' advance notice of the request before the start of employment. Oregon . . . changed to shorten the allowable temporal scope of noncompetes from two years to eighteen months. . . . Hawaii changed its law in 2015 to restrict the use of employee noncompetes for high-tech workers in an attempt to match California's success in developing the Silicon Valley agglomeration economy. Other states . . . [protected] broadcasters in New York, physicians in Massachusetts, [and] used car salesmen in Louisiana.

CHAPTER 12

UNEMPLOYMENT

B. PLANT CLOSINGS

Page 1052. Please add the following to the end of Note 6.

One such state "mass-layoff law," the California WARN Act, provides, unlike the Federal WARN Act, that it applies to temporary layoffs that are as brief as five weeks long. Because such a stoppage is a "layoff" under California law, it triggers the requirement of 60 days' notice to affected employees. See Int'l Brotherhood of Boilermakers v. Nassco Holdings, 17 Cal. App. 5th 1105 (Cal. Ct. App. 2017).

D. UNEMPLOYMENT INSURANCE

3. LEGAL ISSUES IN UNEMPLOYMENT INSURANCE

b. SEPARATIONS

(ii) Discharge for Misconduct

Page 1091. Please insert this case as the third paragraph of Note 1.

Another "run-of-the-mill" discharge-for-misconduct case concerns failure of an employee to meet the employer's absenteeism written policy. In Wisconsin Dept. of Workforce Develop. v. Wisconsin Lab. & Indus. Rev. Comm. & Beres, 2018 WL 3122163 (Wis. June 26, 2018), the Wisconsin Supreme Court held that if an employee violates an employer's written absenteeism policy, that employee engages in "misconduct" and is not eligible for unemployment compensation benefits. More specifically, a written absenteeism policy stated that an employee can be terminated for incurring a single absence during his/her probationary period if he/she does not provide prior notice of the absence. Beres (the former employee) incurred a single absence due to "flu-like" symptoms, did not provide prior notice that she would be absent, and was fired. Even though the Wisconsin statute was more lenient in defining what constitutes misconduct for unemployment compensation purposes, the Court concluded that the pertinent Wisconsin statute (Wis. Stat. § 104.05(e)) allows employers to create and enforce their own written absenteeism policy more strict than the statute, and that if an employee acknowledges receipt of that policy and violates that written policy, the violation constitutes "misconduct."

Page 1098. Please insert this case at the end of Note 4.

But see Wilson v. Mortgage Resource Center, Inc., 888 N.W. 2d 452 (Minn. 2016) (finding that false statements when applying for job is misconduct under exclusive definition provided under state unemployment insurance statute, and therefore employee is not eligible for unemployment insurance when she lost her job on that basis).

c.   CONTINUING ELIGIBILITY

(i)   Availability

Page 1108. Please insert this paragraph as Note 6.

6.   Is an individual "unemployed" while taking unpaid leave under the Family and Medical Leave Act (FMLA)? The Supreme Court of Texas, in Texas Workforce Commission v. Wichita County, 2018 WL 2375140 (Tex. May 25, 2018), found that the employee did not qualify as "unemployed" under the Texas Unemployment Compensation law while she was taking unpaid leave from her job. More specifically, the court found that she was "unemployed" because she clearly met the Act's definition of "totally unemployed"; that is, she was not "perform[ing] services for wages." Tex. Lab. Code § 201.091(a). On the other hand, in response to claims that its holding in the case led to an absurd result, the court pointed out that because eligibility for benefits requires more than unemployed status, it was expressing no opinion on whether an individual on FMLA leave is entitled to unemployment benefits (but at least hinted that most employees on unpaid FMLA leave will not be able to simultaneously obtain unemployment benefits).

CHAPTER 13

RETIREMENT

B. THE PRIVATE PENSION SYSTEM

2. ERISA

b. DEFINED CONTRIBUTION PLANS

Page 1146. Please add new third paragraph in Note 1.

In Osberg v. Foot Locker, 862 F.3d. 198 (2d Cir. 2017), cert. denied, 138 S.Ct. 981 (2018), the company was found by the district court to have violated ERISA by converting to a cash balance pension plan that cut back employee benefits without explaining the changes properly to its employees. On appeal, the parties disputed the proper nature of equitable relief under ERISA section 502(a)(3). The court sided with the employees in reforming the plan to what they should have received before the conversion to the cash balance plan that breached the employer's fiduciary duties, even though this reformation resulted in a windfall to certain plan participants.

Page 1148. Please add new note.

6. About 55 million American workers have no access to an employer-created retirement savings plan. As a solution, several states passed or were considering legislation that would require certain employers or permit certain cities or counties to enroll workers in a state plan. The Obama Department of Labor issued a rule encouraging states to do this. But the Republican Congress and President have now "disapproved" the rule so that "such rule shall have no force or effect." The Senate vote was 50–49. Public Law 115–35, 115th Congress.

c. FIDUCIARY DUTIES UNDER ERISA

Page 1158. Please replace Note 15 with the following.

15. In Fifth Third Bancorp v. Dudenhoeffer, 134 S.Ct. 2459 (2014), the Supreme Court held that fiduciaries' investments in company stock were not entitled to a "presumption of prudence," and instead held that "[t]o state a claim for breach of the duty of prudence on the basis of inside information, a plaintiff must plausibly allege an alternative action that the defendant could have taken that would have been consistent with the securities laws and that a prudent fiduciary in the same circumstances would not have viewed as more likely to harm the fund than to help it." In Amgen Inc. v. Harris, 136 S.Ct. 758 (2016), the Court clarified that the plaintiff bears a significant burden of proposing an alternative course of action so clearly beneficial that a prudent fiduciary could *not* conclude that it would be more likely to harm the fund than to help it.

In Whitley v. BP, P.L.C., 838 F.3d 523 (5th Cir. 2016), former investors of the BP Stock Fund, an employee stock ownership plan (ESOP) comprised primarily of the company's stock, sued the company for breaching their fiduciary duties under ERISA. The Fifth Circuit reversed and remanded the district court's judgment in granting the stockholders' motion to amend the complaint because it found that the amended complaint failed to state a plausible claim under the new pleading standards. Similarly, in Rinehart v. Lehman Bros. Holdings Inc., 817 F.3d 56 (2d Cir. 2016), cert. denied, 137 S.Ct. 1067 (2017) former participants in an employee stock ownership plan (ESOP) who invested exclusively in Lehman's common stock filed suit against the company for breaching their fiduciary duties under ERISA by continuing to permit investment in Lehman stock in circumstances arguably foreshadowing its bankruptcy in 2008. The Second Circuit affirmed the district court's judgment in granting the defendant fiduciaries' motion to dismiss because plaintiffs failed to plead plausibly that defendants breached their ERISA duties. Under *Amgen* standards, the Court found here that a prudent fiduciary could have concluded divesting Lehman stock, or simply holding it without purchasing more, "would do more harm than good."

Page 1158. Please add the following notes.

16. In June 2017, the Supreme Court ruled unanimously that religiously affiliated hospitals can run their pension plans as church plans, which are exempt from ERISA requirements. The ruling reverses the decisions of three federal appeals courts, which had held that a church plan exempt from ERISA requirements must be established by a church. The Supreme Court disagreed, holding that a church plan may include pension plans that are established by an organization that is not a church but is affiliated with a church. The decision permits religious affiliated hospitals to avoid compliance with ERISA and its rules designed to protect the beneficiaries of pension plans. Advocate Health Care Network v. Stapleton, 2017 WL 2407476 (U.S. June 5, 2017).

17. Difficult issues arise with multi-employer plans, which are usually managed by relevant labor unions. See Treasury Department (decision by famous mediator Ken Feinberg) blocking Teamsters' Central States Pension Fund from cutting benefits to retirees to attempt to keep fund solvent. Decades ago, the plan had four active workers contributing for each retiree collecting. Now there are more retirees than active workers. It has about $17 billion in assets and $35 billion in liabilities. The highest compensated retirees get about $2,400 per month. See Wall St. J., May 7, 2016, page B1.

18. Early in 2016, the Obama Department of Labor issued new fiduciary standards for those who provide retirement investment advice. The regulations were meant to protect retirement savers from conflicts of interest faced by brokers and advisers who charge for investment recommendations. With their new fiduciary status, investment managers would have to recommend products that best suit their clients' interests as opposed to those that maximize their own profits.

In Chamber of Commerce of the United States of America v. United States Department of Labor, 885 F.3d 360 (5th Cir. 2018), a divided Fifth

Circuit vacated the Fiduciary Rule. The Fiduciary Rule sought to expand the definition of fiduciary under ERISA section 3(21)(A) to include individuals and entities that provide investment advice for a fee to ERISA-covered plans and their participants and beneficiaries, individual retirement account (IRA) owners, and health savings account (HSA) holders. Reversing an earlier decision by the District Court for the Northern District of Texas, the Fifth Circuit found that DOL exceeded its statutory authority under ERISA in promulgating the Fiduciary rule. The majority decision focused on the DOL's five factor test for determining whether a service provider is an ERISA fiduciary and specifically noted that "[f]or the past forty years, the DOL has considered the hallmarks of an 'investment advice' fiduciary's business to be his 'regular' work on behalf of a client and the client's reliance on that advice as the 'primary basis' for her investment decisions." The majority held the Fiduciary rule was a vast expansion of this historical interpretation that was not authorized by ERISA and in violation of the *Chevron* doctrine—providing for judicial deference to administrative interpretations—and the Administrative Procedure Act (APA). The case vacated the Fiduciary Rule in its entirety and issued a nationwide injunction against its enforcement.

19. In Tibble v. Edison Int'l, 135 S.Ct. 1823 (2015), beneficiaries of a defined-contribution 401(k) retirement savings plan filed a class action suit against the plan fiduciaries, alleging that the employer breached its fiduciary duties by offering higher-priced retail-class mutual funds as plan investments when materially-identical lower-price institutional-class mutual funds were available. After the Supreme Court vacated the Ninth Circuit's decision that ERISA's six-year statute of limitation barred the plaintiffs' claim, the en banc court on remand vacated the district court's judgment in favor of the plan fiduciaries and held that the duty of prudence required defendants to reevaluate investments periodically and to take into account their power to obtain favorable investment products, particularly when those products were substantially identical—other than their lower cost—to products they had already selected. Tibble v. Edison Int'l, 843 F.3d 1187 (9th Cir. 2016).

e.   FEDERAL PREEMPTION OF STATE LAW

Page 1163. Please add as new notes.

3.   The ex-wife of a military retiree filed a motion to enforce a divorce decree that granted her 50% of her ex-husband's military retirement pay (MRP). After he waived a portion of MRP in order to collect service-related disability benefits, the former wife's share was reduced. The MRP reduction reduced the MRP amount by about $250 per month, thus $125 each for husband and former wife. (The veteran made that decision because retirement benefits are taxable and disability benefits are not.) The Arizona Supreme Court ruled that the divorce award from family court should survive the reduction in the husband's MRP. The U.S. Supreme Court reversed, deciding unanimously that the federal statute allowing states to treat as community property and divide at divorce a veteran's MRP payments exempts from this grant of permission any amount that the federal government deducts as a result of a waiver that the veteran must make in order to receive disability benefits. Howell v. Howell, 136 S.Ct. 1704 (2017).

4. Although private pension benefits under ERISA are nonforfeitable in *most* cases, murder under so-called state slayer statues is one where pension rights can be lost. See Pension Fund v. Miscevic, 880 F.3d 927 (7th Cir. 2018) (holding that ERISA does not preempt Illinois state slayer statute which barred participant's wife from recovering participant's pension benefits after she was found not guilty of murdering him by reason of insanity).

3. GOVERNMENT PENSIONS AS CONTRACT

Page 1178. Please insert on bottom of page.

In re Pension Reform Litigation (Heaton v. Quinn)
32 N.E.3d 1 (Ill. 2015).

■ JUSTICE KARMEIER delivered the judgment of the court, with opinion.

At issue on this appeal is the constitutionality of Public Act 98–599 (eff. June 1, 2014), which amends the Illinois Pension Code by reducing retirement annuity benefits for individuals who first became members of four of Illinois' five State-funded pension systems prior to January 1, 2011. Members of the retirement systems affected by Public Act 98–599 and groups representing those members brought five separate actions challenging the validity of the new law on the grounds that it violated numerous provisions of the Illinois Constitution of 1970, including article XIII, section 5 (Ill. Const. 1970, art. XIII, § 5), popularly known as the pension protection clause.

* * *

Illinois has established five State-funded retirement systems for public employees. * * * These systems provide traditional defined benefit plans under which members earn specific benefits based on their years of service, income and age. All are subject to the pension protection clause of our state constitution, which provides: "Membership in any pension or retirement system of the State, any unit of local government or school district, or any agency or instrumentality thereof, shall be an enforceable contractual relationship, the benefits of which shall not be diminished or impaired." Ill. Const. 1970, art. XIII, § 5.

Among the benefits which members of the five State-funded retirement systems are entitled to receive are retirement annuities. The amount of a member's retirement annuity and how soon a member is eligible to begin receiving annuity payments depends on when the member first began making contributions into one of the retirement systems. Members who first contributed prior to January 1, 2011, receive what are known as "Tier 1" annuity benefits. Members first contributing on or after January 1, 2011, receive a lower level of benefits designated as "Tier 2." Public Act 98–599, the legislation challenged in this case, is directed primarily at Tier 1 annuities and is limited in its application to benefits earned under the [four of the pension plans]. Annuities paid to judges under the JRS system were intentionally excluded from the law and are not affected by it.

Tier 1 retirement annuity benefits and eligibility requirements differ somewhat between the various systems. Because they all operate in approximately the same way, however, we will choose just one, SERS, to illustrate their basic features.

Members of [one plan] are eligible to retire at age 60 if they have at least eight years of credited service. They may retire with full benefits at any age if their age plus years of service credit equal 85. They are also eligible to retire if they are between the ages of 55 and 60 and have at least 25 years of credited service, but their benefit will be reduced by half of 1% for each month they are under the age of 60.

The amount of the retirement annuity benefit under SERS is calculated based on (1) the member's final average compensation, which is the average monthly compensation they received during their highest-paid 48 consecutive months of service over the previous ten years, (2) their total credited service, and (3) a multiplier, which changes depending on (a) whether or not the member is also covered by Social Security or (b) qualifies for an "alternative retirement annuity" (applicable to, *e.g.*, pilots and state policemen). For members who do have Social Security and are not subject to the alternative retirement annuity rules, the multiplier is 1.67% per year of credited service. Accordingly, a member of SERS who is eligible to retire, who has also paid into Social Security, and who has final average compensation of $1800 per month and 30 years of credited service will receive a retirement annuity of $901.80 per month (30 x .0167 x $1800).

SERS members may earn a retirement annuity of up to 75% of their final average compensation, although for members covered by Social Security, it would take nearly 45 years of State service to do so. These annuity payments are subject to 3% automatic annual increases beginning after the member's first full year of retirement, except that some members who retire before 60 and do not meet the rule of 85 will not receive the increases until they turn 60 and have been retired at least one full year. The annual annuity adjustments are built-in to the pension benefit and are not tied to the cost of living. As a result, the real value of annuities may either increase or erode depending on economic conditions, notwithstanding the adjustments.

Funding to pay benefits under each of Illinois' five State-funded systems is derived from three basic sources: contributions by the State through appropriation by the General Assembly; contributions by or on behalf of members based on their salaries; and income, interest and dividends derived from retirement fund deposits and investments. The contributions to the systems by or on behalf of members of the systems have not been problematic. There is no dispute that employees have paid their full share as required by law at all times relevant to this litigation. That has not been the case with respect to the contributions owed by the General Assembly.

For as long as there have been public pension systems in Illinois, there has been tension between the government's responsibility for funding those systems, on the one hand, and the costs of supporting governmental programs and providing governmental services, on the other. In the resulting political give and take, public pensions have chronically suffered. As long ago as 1917, a report commissioned by the General Assembly characterized the condition of State and municipal pension systems as "one of insolvency" and "moving toward a crisis" because of financial provisions which were "entirely inadequate for paying the stipulated pensions when due."

* * *

Concern over ongoing funding deficiencies and the attendant threat to the security of retirees in public pension systems eventually led directly to adoption of article XIII, section 5, the pension protection clause, when the new constitution was adopted in 1970.

* * *

Despite the consistent warnings from the Pension Laws Commission, the current budgeting of pension costs necessary to ensure the financial stability of these funds, the General Assembly has failed to meet its commitments to finance the pension obligations on a sound basis.

* * *

The solution proposed by the drafters and ultimately approved by the people of Illinois was to protect the benefits of membership in public pension systems not by dictating specific funding levels, but by safeguarding the benefits themselves. Delegate Green explained that the pension protection clause does this in two ways: "[i]t first mandates a contractual relationship between the employer and the employee; and secondly, it mandates the General Assembly not to impair or diminish these rights." Subsequent comments by other delegates reaffirmed that the provision was designed to confer contractual protection on the benefits of membership in public retirement systems and afford beneficiaries, pensioners or their dependents "'a basic protection against abolishing their rights completely or changing the terms of their rights after they have embarked upon the employment— to lessen them."

* * *

By the end of June, 2013, the five State-funded retirement systems contained a total of only 41.1% of the funding necessary to meet their accrued liabilities based on the market value of fund assets. The funding rate was thus nearly unchanged from the 41.8% funding rate prior to ratification of the 1970 Constitution and its pension protection clause.

* * *

Following downgrades in the State's credit rating and facing the prospect that its credit rating would be reduced even further, the General Assembly engaged in heated and protracted debate over possible legislative strategies for dealing with the State's fiscal problems through further changes to its pension obligations. After numerous failed attempts to reach consensus, the General Assembly ultimately enacted what became Public Act 98–599, the legislation challenged in this case.

Introduced as Senate Bill 1 and passed during the legislature's fall, 2013, "veto session," Public Act 98–599 was described as an attempt to address the State's large debts and deficits, plummeting credit ratings, and imperiled discretionary spending programs "that are essential to the people of Illinois" and to help shore up the long-term fiscal stability of both the State and its retirement systems. The mechanism chosen under the Act to accomplish those purposes was restructuring State-funded retirement systems. The law does not pertain to all five of the State-funded retirement systems, however. As noted earlier, JRS, the Judges Retirement System, was deliberately excluded.

* * *

The Act provides a limited number of Tier 1 plan participants with the opportunity, at a future date, to participate in a defined contribution plan. It affords a nominal reduction in the percentage of their salaries Tier 1 plan participants are required to contribute toward the employee share of annuity costs. Going forward, it bars persons hired by certain nongovernmental organizations from participating in the public pension system and prohibits new hires from using accumulated sick or vacation time to boost their pension benefits. Public Act 98–599 also eliminates the duty of employers to engage in collective bargaining or interest arbitration "over matters affected by the changes, the impact of changes, and the implementation of changes" made to the [pension] systems by the new law.

The centerpiece of Public Act 98–599, however, is a comprehensive set of provisions designed to reduce annuity benefits for members entitled to Tier 1 benefits, i.e., members who belonged to those systems prior to January 1, 2011. The new law utilizes five different mechanisms for achieving this goal. First, it delays, by up to five years, when members under the age of 46 are eligible to begin receiving their retirement annuities. Second, with certain exceptions and qualifications, it caps the maximum salary that may be considered when calculating the amount of a member's retirement annuity. Third, it jettisons the current provisions under which retirees receive flat 3% annual increases to their annuities and replaces them with a system under which annual annuity increases are determined according to a variable formula and are limited. Fourth, it completely eliminates at least one and up to five annual annuity increases depending on the age of the pension system member at the time of the Act's effective date. Finally, with respect to the TRS and SURS systems, the Act also alters how the base annuity amount is determined for purposes of what is known as the "money purchase" formula, something available to members of those two systems who began employment prior to July 1, 2005, as an alternative to the standard formula for calculating pensions. Because of this change, which involves use of a different interest rate, affected members will have smaller base pensions.

* * *

The first issue, whether Public Act 98–599's reduction of retirement annuity benefits violates this State's pension protection clause, is easily resolved. The pension protection clause clearly states: "[m]embership in any pension or retirement system of the State * * * shall be an enforceable contractual relationship, *the benefits of which shall not be diminished or impaired.*" This clause has been construed by our court on numerous occasions, most recently in *Kanerva v. Weems*, 2014 IL 115811. We held in that case that the clause means precisely what it says: "if something qualifies as a benefit of the enforceable contractual relationship resulting from membership in one of the State's pension or retirement systems, it cannot be diminished or impaired."

This construction of article XIII, section 5, was not a break from prior law. To the contrary, it was a reaffirmation of principles articulated by this court and the   appellate court on numerous occasions since the 1970 Constitution took effect. Under article XIII, section 5, members of pension plans subject to its provisions have a legally enforceable right to receive the benefits they have been promised. The protections afforded to such benefits by article XIII, section 5 attach once an individual first embarks upon employment in a position covered by a public retirement system, not when the employee ultimately retires. Accordingly, once an individual begins work and becomes a member of a public retirement system, any subsequent changes to the Pension Code that would diminish the benefits conferred by membership in the retirement system cannot be applied to that individual.

* * *

That the annuity reduction provisions of Public Act 98–599 violate the pension protection clause's prohibition against the diminishment of the benefits of membership in a State-funded retirement system is one the State has now all but conceded. After this court reaffirmed in *Kanerva v. Weems* that the pension protection clause means precisely what it says, the State shifted its focus to an argument it did not raise and we did not consider in *Kanerva*. The State's position now rests on its affirmative defense that funding for the pension systems and State finances in general have become so dire that the General Assembly is authorized, even compelled, to invoke the State's "reserved sovereign powers," i.e., its police powers, to override the rights and protections afforded by article XIII, section 5, of the Illinois Constitution in the interests of the greater public good. This argument must also fail.

The circumstances presented by this case are not unique. Economic conditions are cyclical and expected, and fiscal difficulties have confronted the State before. In the midst of previous downturns, the State or political subdivisions of the State have attempted to reduce or eliminate expenditures protected by the Illinois Constitution, as the General Assembly is attempting to do with Public Act 98–599. Whenever those efforts have been challenged in court, we have clearly and consistently found them to be improper.

* * *

The State seeks to avoid this conclusion by arguing that because membership in public retirement systems is an enforceable contractual relationship under article XIII, section 5, it should be subject to the same limitations as all other contractual rights; that under "a century and a half of federal and state law defining contractual relationships," these rights remain subject to modification—even invalidation—by the General Assembly through the exercise of the State's police power; and that the reduction in retirement annuity benefits under Public Act 98–599 is a valid exercise of police power because it is necessary and reasonable to secure the State's fiscal health and the well being of its citizens.

This argument was rejected by the circuit court. We reject it as well. As a preliminary matter, the precedent on which the State relies does not involve the pension protection clause under article XIII, section 5. It arises, instead, under article I, section 16, and that provision's counterpart in the United States Constitution. Those provisions, which are popularly referred to as the "contracts clause," provide that the State shall not pass any "law impairing the obligation of contracts."

* * *

This is not surprising. While impairment of a contract may survive scrutiny under the contracts clause if reasonable and necessary to serve an important public purpose, " '[t]he severity of the impairment measures the height of the hurdle the state legislation must clear.' " Changes in the factors used to compute public pension benefits constitute an impairment which is "obviously substantial."

The United States Supreme Court has made clear that the United States Constitution "bar[s] Government from forcing some people alone to bear public burdens which, in all fairness and justice, should be borne by the public as a whole." Through Public Act 98–599, however, the General Assembly addressed the financial challenges facing our State by doing just that. It made no effort to distribute the burdens evenly among Illinoisans. It did not even attempt to distribute the burdens evenly among those with whom it has contractual relationships. Although it is undisputed that many vendors face delays in payment, the terms of their contracts are unchanged, and under the State Prompt Payment Act, vendors are actually entitled to additional compensation in the form of statutory interest if their bills are not paid within specified periods. In no sense is this comparable to the situation confronted by members of public retirement systems under Public Act 98–599, which, if allowed to take effect, would actually negate substantive terms of their contractual relationships and reduce the benefits due and payable to them in a real and absolute way. Under all of these circumstances, it is clear that the State could prove no set of circumstances that would satisfy the contracts clause. Its resort to the contracts clause to support its police powers argument must therefore be rejected as a matter of law.

* * *

Given the history of article XIII, section 5, and the language that was ultimately adopted, we therefore have no possible basis for interpreting the provision to mean that its protections can be overridden if the General Assembly deems it appropriate, as it sometimes can be under the contracts clause. To confer such authority on the legislature through judicial fiat would require that we ignore the plain language of the constitution and rewrite it to include "restrictions and limitations that the drafters did not express and the citizens of Illinois did not approve."   Indeed,   accepting   the   State's   position   that   reducing retirement benefits is justified by economic circumstances would require that we allow the legislature to do the very thing the pension protection clause was designed to prevent it from doing. Article XIII, section 5, would be rendered a nullity.

The State protests that this conclusion is tantamount to holding that the State has surrendered its sovereign authority, something it may not do. The State is incorrect. Article XIII, section 5, is in no sense a surrender of any attribute of sovereignty. Rather, it is a statement by the people of Illinois, made in the clearest possible terms, that the authority of the legislature does not include the power to diminish or impair the benefits of membership in a public retirement system. This is a restriction the people of Illinois had every right to impose.

* * *

The financial challenges facing state and local governments in Illinois are well known and significant. In ruling as we have today, we do not mean to minimize the gravity of the State's problems or the magnitude of the difficulty facing our elected representatives. It is our obligation, however, just as it is theirs, to ensure that the law is followed. That is true at all times. It is especially important in times of crisis when, as this case demonstrates, even clear principles and long-standing precedent   are threatened. Crisis is not an excuse to abandon the rule of law. It is a summons to defend it. How we respond is the measure of our commitment to the principles of justice we are sworn to uphold.

More than two centuries ago, as adoption of the Constitution of the United States was being considered by the citizens of our new nation, James Madison wrote:

> "If men were angels, no government would be necessary. * * *
> In framing a government which is to be administered by men over men, the great difficulty lies in this: you must first enable the government to control the governed; and in the next place oblige it to control itself." James Madison, Federalist No. 51 (1788).

Obliging the government to control itself is what we are called upon to do today. The Constitution of Illinois and the precedent of our court admit of only one conclusion: the annuity reduction provisions of Public Act 98–599 enacted by the legislature and signed into law by the Governor violate article XIII, section 5's express prohibition against the diminishment of the benefits of membership in public retirement systems. The circuit court was therefore entirely correct when it declared those provisions void and unenforceable.

NOTES

1.   This decision was followed in 2016 by a case reaching the same conclusion regarding Chicago's obligation to keep its pension promises. Jones v. Municipal Employees' Annuity & Benefit Fund, 50 N.E.3d 596 (2016). On the same day, the same Supreme Court refused to enforce an arbitration decision directing the state to pay a 2% wage increase to state employees covered by a multiyear collective bargaining agreement in State v. AFSCME, 51 N.E.3d 738 (Ill. 2016). It vacated the award and held that because the state's constitution and statutes provide a well-defined and dominant public policy in which collective bargaining agreements are subject to the appropriation power of the State (i.e., the State has the ability to appropriate and expend public funds), the arbitration award violated this public policy.

Further, the Illinois state court of appeals distinguished *Jones* in Pisani v. City of Springfield, 73 N.E.3d 129 (Ill. Ct. App. 2017), where it held that the city's elimination of a pension-spiking opportunity did not violate the state constitution's pension protection clause.

2.   Michigan imposed substantial employee contribution charges in the pension plan and made changes in the retiree benefit plan for public school employees. The Michigan Supreme Court found no contract clause or other constitutional violation. AFT Michigan v. State, 866 N.W.2d 782 (Mich. 2015). The Oregon Supreme Court overturned changes in public pensions as they affected benefits earned before particular dates in 2013, but found constitutional the reduction of retiree COLA payments prospectively from 2013. Moro v. State, 351 P.3d 1 (Or. 2015). The New Hampshire Supreme Court held that the state did not violate state and federal constitutional clauses when it raised contribution levels for pensions. Prof'l Fire Fighters of N.H. v. State, 107 A.3d 1229 (N.H. 2014).

In Berg v. Christie, 137 A.3d 1143 (N.J. 2016), retired government employees filed suit against various New Jersey state defendants for suspending state pension cost-of-living adjustments (COLAs) in 2011, alleging that plaintiffs had contractual, statutory, and constitutional rights to pension COLAs. The Supreme Court of New Jersey held that although the state legislature enacted a non-forfeitable-right statute in 1997, the proof of unequivocal intent to create a non-forfeitable right to yet-unreceived COLAs is lacking, and the state legislature retained its inherent sovereign right to act in the best judgment of the public interest and to enact legislation suspending further COLAs.

3.   Since 1996, retired employees of the City and County of San Francisco ("City") have been eligible to receive a supplemental COLA as part of their pension benefits when the retirement fund's earnings from the previous year exceeded projected earnings. Protect Our Benefits, a political action committee representing the interests of retired City employees, sought to invalidate a 2011 amendment to the city's Charter to condition the payment of the supplemental COLA on the retirement fund being "fully funded" based on the market value of the assets for the previous year as an impairment of a vested contractual pension right under the contract clauses of the federal and state constitutions. The California Court of Appeals held that the 2011 amendment may be constitutionally applied to employees who retired before the 1996 initiative establishing the supplemental COLA, but not to current employees or those who retired after the 1996 initiative. It found that employees who retired before 1996 do not have the same vested rights based on the contract in effect during their employment because they did not have a contractual expectation while in service that they would receive a supplement COLA. Protect Our Benefits v. City & Cnty. of San Francisco, 185 Cal. Rptr. 3d 410 (Cal. Ct. App. 2015).

Current county employees brought suit to halt a legislative amendment that would implement a revised formula for calculating retirement income to respond to the concerns of "pension spiking," by which some public employees attempt to inflate their income and retirement benefits. The California Court of Appeals upheld the lower court's finding that the state legislature did not act impermissibly because although a public employee has a vested right to a pension, that right is only to a "reasonable" pension, not an immutable entitlement to the most optimal formula of calculating the pension. As long as the legislature's modifications do not deprive the employee of a "reasonable" pension, there is no constitutional violation of the employee's contractual rights. Marin Ass'n of Public Employees v. Marin Cnty. Employees' Retirement Ass'n, 206 Cal. Rptr. 3d 365 (Cal. Ct. App. 2016).

4. In a non-pension case involving a life insurance policy beneficiary designation, the United States Supreme Court found that Minnesota's automatic-revocation-on-divorce statute that permits divorce alone to annul a life insurance policy in favor of the former spouse did not violate the Contracts Clause. This is because the Court found that the Minnesota did not substantially impair pre-existing contractual arrangements. Only Justice Gorsuch dissented. Sveen v. Melin, 138 S.Ct. 1815 (2018).

C. SOCIAL SECURITY RETIREMENT BENEFITS

3. GENDER DISCRIMINATION IN SOCIAL SECURITY

Page 1191. Please insert at end of Note 3.

Accord MacNeil v. Berryhill, 869 F.3d 109 (2d Cir. 2017) (under New York state intestacy law, finding that child conceived from frozen sperm of father who died 11 years earlier not entitled to Social Security survivor benefits).

D. RETIREE HEALTH CARE

Page 1202. Please insert at end of page.

M&G Polymers USA v. Tackett
135 S.Ct. 926 (2015).

■ JUSTICE THOMAS delivered the opinion of the Court.

This case arises out of a disagreement between a group of retired employees and their former employer about the meaning of certain expired collective-bargaining agreements. The retirees (and their former union) claim that these agreements created a right to lifetime contribution-free health care benefits for retirees, their surviving spouses, and their dependents. The employer, for its part, claims that those provisions terminated when the agreements expired. The United States Court of Appeals for the Sixth Circuit sided with the retirees, relying on its conclusion * * * that retiree health care benefits are unlikely to be left up to future negotiations. We granted certiorari and now conclude that such reasoning is incompatible with ordinary principles of contract law. We therefore vacate the judgment of the Court of Appeals and remand for it to apply ordinary principles of contract law in the first instance.

Respondents * * * worked at (and retired from) the Point Pleasant Polyester Plant in Apple Grove, West Virginia. During their employment, respondent United Steel, Paper and Forestry, Rubber, Manufacturing, Energy, Allied Industrial and Service Workers International Union, AFL-CIO-CLC, or its predecessor unions, represented them in collective bargaining. Tackett and Pyles retired in 1996, and Conley retired in 1998. They represent a class of retired employees from the Plant, along with their surviving spouses and other dependents. Petitioner M&G Polymers USA, LLC, is the current owner of the Plant.

When M&G purchased the Plant in 2000, it entered a master collective-bargaining agreement and a Pension, Insurance, and Service Award Agreement (P & I agreement) with the Union, generally similar to agreements the Union had negotiated with M&G's predecessor. The P & I agreement provided for retiree health care benefits as follows:

"Employees who retire on or after January 1, 1996 and who are eligible for and receiving a monthly pension under the 1993 Pension Plan . . . whose full years of attained age and full years of attained continuous service . . . at the time of retirement equals 95 or more points will receive a full Company contribution towards the cost of [health care] benefits described in this Exhibit B-1 . . . . Employees who have less than 95 points at the time of retirement will receive a reduced Company contribution. The Company contribution will be reduced by 2% for every point less than 95. Employees will be required to pay the balance of the health care contribution, as estimated by the Company annually in advance, for the [health care] benefits described in this Exhibit B-1. Failure to pay the required medical contribution will result in cancellation of coverage."

Exhibit B-1, which described the health care benefits at issue, opened with the following durational clause: "Effective January 1, 1998, and for the duration of this Agreement thereafter, the Employer will provide the following program of hospital benefits, hospital-medical benefits, surgical benefits and prescription drug benefits for eligible employees and their dependents. . . . " The P & I agreement provided for renegotiation of its terms in three years.

In December 2006, M&G announced that it would begin requiring retirees to contribute to the cost of their health care benefits. Respondent retirees, on behalf of themselves and others similarly situated, sued M&G and related entities, alleging that the decision to require these contributions breached both the collective-bargaining agreement and the P & I agreement, in violation of § 301 of the Labor Management Relations Act, 1947 (LMRA) and [ERISA]. Specifically, the retirees alleged that M&G had promised to provide lifetime contribution-free health care benefits for them, their surviving spouses, and their dependents. They pointed to the language in the 2000 P & I agreement providing that employees with a certain level of seniority "will receive a full Company contribution towards the cost of [health care] benefits described in . . . Exhibit B-1." The retirees alleged that, with this promise, M&G had created a vested right to such benefits that continued beyond the expiration of the 2000 P & I agreement.

* * *

This case is about the interpretation of collective-bargaining agreements that define rights to welfare benefits plans.

* * *

ERISA treats [pension plans and welfare benefit plans] differently. Although ERISA imposes elaborate minimum funding and vesting standards for pension plans, it explicitly exempts welfare benefits plans from those rules. Welfare benefits plans must be "established and maintained pursuant to a written instrument," § 1102(a)(1), but "[e]mployers or other plan sponsors are generally free under ERISA, for any reason at any time, to adopt, modify, or terminate welfare plans." As we have previously recognized, "[E]mployers have large leeway to design disability and other welfare plans as they see fit." And, we have observed, the rule that contractual "provisions ordinarily should be enforced as written is especially appropriate when enforcing an ERISA [welfare benefits] plan." That is because the "focus on the written terms of the plan is the linchpin of a system that is not so complex that administrative costs, or litigation expenses, unduly discourage employers from offering [welfare benefits] plans in the first place."

We interpret collective-bargaining agreements, including those establishing ERISA plans, according to ordinary principles of contract law, at least when those principles are not inconsistent with federal labor policy. "In this endeavor, as with any other contract, the parties' intentions control." "Where the words of a contract in writing are clear and unambiguous, its meaning is to be ascertained in accordance with its plainly expressed intent."

In this case, the Court of Appeals applied the *Yard-Man* inferences to conclude that, in the absence of extrinsic evidence to the contrary, the provisions of the contract indicated an intent to vest retirees with lifetime benefits. As we now explain, those inferences conflict with ordinary principles of contract law.

The Court of Appeals has long insisted that its *Yard-Man* inferences are drawn from ordinary contract law. In *Yard-Man* itself, the court purported to apply "traditional rules for contractual interpretation." The court first concluded that the provision governing retiree insurance benefits—which stated only that the employer "will provide" such benefits—was ambiguous as to the duration of those benefits. To resolve that ambiguity, it looked to other provisions of the agreement. The agreement included provisions for terminating active employees' insurance benefits in the case of layoffs and for terminating benefits for a retiree's spouse and dependents in case of the retiree's death before the expiration of the collective-bargaining agreement, but no provision specifically addressed the duration of retiree health care benefits. From the existence of these termination provisions and the absence of a termination provision specifically addressing retiree benefits, the court inferred an intent to vest those retiree benefits for life.

* * *

We disagree with the Court of Appeals' assessment that the inferences applied in *Yard-Man* and its progeny represent ordinary principles of contract law.

As an initial matter, *Yard-Man* violates ordinary contract principles by placing a thumb on the scale in favor of vested retiree benefits in all collective-bargaining agreements. That rule has no basis in ordinary principles of contract law. And it distorts the attempt "to ascertain the intention of *the parties.*" *Yard-Man*'s assessment of likely behavior in collective bargaining is too speculative and too far removed from the context of any particular contract to be useful in discerning the parties' intention.

* * *

The Court of Appeals also failed even to consider the traditional principle that courts should not construe ambiguous writings to create lifetime promises. The court recognized that "traditional rules of contractual interpretation require a clear manifestation of intent before conferring a benefit or obligation," but asserted that "the duration of the benefit once clearly conferred is [not] subject to this stricture." In stark contrast to this assertion, however, the court later applied that very stricture to noncollectively bargained contracts offering retiree benefits. The different treatment of these two types of employment contracts only underscores *Yard-Man*'s deviation from ordinary principles of contract law.

Similarly, the Court of Appeals failed to consider the traditional principle that "contractual obligations will cease, in the ordinary course, upon termination of the bargaining agreement." That principle does not preclude the conclusion that the parties intended to vest lifetime benefits for retirees. Indeed, we have already recognized that "a collective-bargaining agreement [may] provid[e] in explicit terms that certain benefits continue after the agreement's expiration." But when a contract is silent as to the duration of retiree benefits, a court may not infer that the parties intended those benefits to vest for life.

There is no doubt that *Yard-Man* and its progeny affected the outcome here. As in its previous decisions, the Court of Appeals here cited the "context of . . . labor-management negotiations" and reasoned that the Union likely would not have agreed to language ensuring its members a "full Company contribution" if the company could change the level of that contribution. It similarly concluded that the tying of eligibility for health care benefits to receipt of pension benefits suggested an intent to vest health care benefits. And it framed its analysis from beginning to end in light of the principles it announced in *Yard-Man* and its progeny.

We reject the *Yard-Man* inferences as inconsistent with ordinary principles of contract law. But because "[t]his Court is one of final review, not of first view," the Court of Appeals should be the first to review the agreements at issue under the correct legal principles. We vacate the judgment of the Court of Appeals and remand the case for that court to apply ordinary principles of contract law in the first instance.

■ JUSTICE GINSBURG, with whom JUSTICE BREYER, JUSTICE SOTOMAYOR, and JUSTICE KAGAN join, concurring.

Today's decision rightly holds that courts must apply ordinary contract principles, shorn of presumptions, to determine whether retiree health-care benefits survive the expiration of a collective-bargaining agreement. Under the "cardinal principle" of contract interpretation, "the intention of the parties, to be gathered from the whole instrument, must prevail." To determine what the contracting parties intended, a court must examine the entire agreement in light of relevant industry-specific "customs, practices, usages, and terminology." When the intent of the parties is unambiguously expressed in the contract, that expression controls, and the court's inquiry should proceed no further. But when the contract is ambiguous, a court may consider extrinsic evidence to determine the intentions of the parties.

Contrary to M&G's assertion, no rule requires "clear and express" language in order to show that parties intended health-care benefits to vest. "[C]onstraints upon the employer after the expiration date of a collective-bargaining agreement," we have observed, may be derived from the agreement's "explicit terms," but they "may arise as well from . . . implied terms of the expired agreement."

On remand, the Court of Appeals should examine the entire agreement to determine whether the parties intended retiree health-care benefits to vest. Because the retirees have a vested, lifetime right to a monthly pension, a provision stating that retirees "will receive" health-care benefits if they are "receiving a monthly pension" is relevant to this examination. So is a "survivor benefits" clause instructing that if a retiree dies, her surviving spouse will "continue to receive [the retiree's health-care] benefits . . . until death or remarriage." If, after considering all relevant contractual language in light of industry practices, the Court of Appeals concludes that the contract is ambiguous, it may turn to extrinsic evidence—for example, the parties' bargaining history. The Court of Appeals, however, must conduct the foregoing inspection without *Yard-Man*'s "thumb on the scale in favor of vested retiree benefits."

Because I understand the Court's opinion to be consistent with these basic rules of contract interpretation, I join it.

NOTES

1. Although *M&G Polymers* remains undecided after the latest Sixth Circuit decision, Tackett v. M&G Polymers, 811 F.3d 204 (6th Cir. 2016), remanding the matter to the district court to make more factual determinations using "ordinary principles of contract law," the Supreme

Court provided some guidance concerning the meaning of "ordinary principles of contract law" in CNH Industrial N.V. v. Reese, 138 S.Ct. 761 (2018) (per curiam). In *CNH Industrial*, the Court thought the contract straightforward that no lifetime retiree health benefits vested.

> Shorn of *Yard-Man* inferences, this case is straightforward. The 1998 agreement contained a general durational clause that applied to all benefits, unless the agreement specified otherwise. No provision specified that the health care benefits were subject to a different durational clause. The agreement stated that the health benefits plan "r[an] concurrently" with the collective-bargaining agreement, tying the health care benefits to the duration of the rest of the agreement. If the parties meant to vest health care benefits for life, they easily could have said so in the text. But they did not. And they specified that their agreement "dispose[d] of any and all bargaining issues" between them. Thus, the only reasonable interpretation of the 1998 agreement is that the health care benefits expired when the collective-bargaining agreement expired in May 2004. "When the intent of the parties is unambiguously expressed in the contract, that expression controls, and the court's inquiry should proceed no further."

See also International Union, United Automobile Workers v. Kelsey-Hayes Co., 854 F.3d 862 (6th Cir. 2017) (2–1 that union contract meant to promise retiree medical benefits for life), cert. granted, judgment vacated in light of CNH Industrial N.V. v. Reese, 138 S.Ct. 761 (2018); Cole v. Meritor, Inc., 855 F.3d 695 (6th Cir. 2017) (contract did not create lifetime health benefits).

2. The Michigan Supreme Court found no constitutional violations in changes made to the retiree benefits plan for public school employees. The court also upheld changes to the pension plan. AFT Michigan v. State, 866 N.W.2d 782 (Mich. 2015).

3. In Gallo v. Moen Inc., 813 F.3d 265 (6th Cir. 2016), retirees and union filed suit against employer, seeking declaration that collective bargaining agreements (CBAs) entitled retirees to vested healthcare benefits for life. The Sixth Circuit reversed the district court's ruling in order to rule consistently with *M&G Polymers USA* and held that under the "ordinary rules of contract law" without an inference in favor of vesting healthcare benefits for life, a series of CBAs cannot be interpreted as a lifetime guarantee of unalterable healthcare benefits to retirees and their dependents.

4. Because retiree health benefits do not vest like pension benefits under ERISA, the Sixth Circuit found that although Honeywell had promised retiree health benefits previously in the last collective bargaining contract, once Honeywell sold the plant and that contract expired, ERISA permitted the company to stop paying for its former employees' retiree healthcare. Watkins v. Honeywell, 875 F.3d 321 (6th Cir. 2017). What incentives do you see this ruling providing to covered employers looking to unload large retiree health care obligations associated with previous union contracts?